Y0-AVA-478

People Around Jesus

PEOPLE AROUND JESUS

Walter A. Kortrey

A PILGRIM PRESS BOOK
from United Church Press, Philadelphia

Copyright © 1974 United Church Press
All Rights Reserved

No part of this publication may be reproduced, stored in a retrieval system, or transmitted in any form or by any means, electronic, mechanical, photocopying, recording, or otherwise, without the prior permission of the publisher.

Library of Congress Cataloging in Publication Data

Kortrey, Walter A 1923-
  People around Jesus.

  "A Pilgrim Press book."
  1. Jesus Christ—Friends and associates. I. Title.
BS2430.K65   225.9'22 [B]   74-16400
ISBN 0-8298-0288-6

With the exception of "Followers at a Distance," the material for Parts I-V is reprinted by permission from *The Lutheran* © 1973. Some of the essays have been revised by the author for publication in this book.

  The scripture quotations (unless otherwise indicated) are from the Today's English Version of the New Testament. Copyright © American Bible Society, 1966, 1971.

United Church Press, 1505 Race Street
Philadelphia, Pennsylvania 19102

Contents

Intentions 6
Who Is Jesus? 8

I. Outer-circle Disciples 15
Followers at a Distance 16
The Quiet One 17
John the Baptist 20
Simon the Zealot 23
The Bethphage Disciple 26
The Emmaus Disciples 29

II. Jesus with Children and Youth 33
Jesus with Children and Youth 34
The Boy with His Lunch 36
The Rich Young Man 40
Nathanael, the Young Apostle 43

III. The Sick and the Sorrowing 47
The Healing Jesus 48
Bartimaeus, the Blind Man 50
The Centurion and His Servant 53
The Ungrateful Lepers 56

IV. Jesus and Women 61
Jesus and Women 62
Mary, His Mother 64
Mary Magdalene 67
Salome, the Mother of James and John 70
Martha of Bethany 73
The Canaanite Woman 76
The Woman at the Well 79
The Widow of Nain 82

V. The Outsiders 85
Friends and Foes Beyond the Fringe 86
Zacchaeus, Low Man on Top 88
Nicodemus, Hidden Disciple 91
Malchus, the Wounded Enemy 94
Simon of Cyrene, the Crossbearer 97

VI. Disciples-Come-Lately 101
Faith Makes the Difference 102
Paul, the Apostle 103
The Disciple in Your Mirror 105

Helps for Further Study 109
A Shared Bible Study Guide
  for PEOPLE AROUND JESUS 110
The Study 114

About the Author 128

Intentions

Christians are, by definition, Christ-followers, Christ-believers, Christ-witnesses. They do not walk in the footsteps of an abstract idea. Their faith does not rest in theological formulas and credal statements. They are not the spokesmen for an ecclesiastical institution or a liturgical tradition. Christians follow a person, *the Person*, Jesus of Nazareth, who lived, boy and man, in Palestine centuries ago and showed in his life and death and resurrection that he was, that he *is*, God with us.

We follow Jesus. We believe *in* Jesus. He shows us the life-style that God would have us live. He accuses us in our sin. He forgives us and, in his love, he redeems us. He, by his indwelling Spirit, leads us to faith. Convicted by Jesus the Christ and saved by his free grace, we proclaim *him*. We are *his* spokesmen. Christians are Christ-followers, Christ-believers, Christ-witnesses.

This being so, it follows, doesn't it, that Christians are Christ-learners? We need to know who he is, what he has done, how he has loved. We need to learn Jesus. In a deeply personal way, we must come into a reverent familiarity with him.

The simple premise of this little book is that one of the best ways to learn Jesus is to see him through the eyes of those who knew him and know him. The people around Jesus in the New Testament and in our daily lives, especially some of the little-known, anonymous ones, have much to show and tell us about him. This study is not, in any sense, a critical examination of New Testament texts. We have sought to be careful in interpretation and faithful to the conclusions of most recognized New Testament scholarship, but the mood of the book is intentionally personal and pastoral in character. It is written in an informal, conversational style that most people should find easy to read and understand. In some of the stories, imagination informed by history and personal experience with people has been used to amplify the scant information provided in the Gospel texts.

I hope that seeking Christians will find in these "people stories" light reading that edifies while it entertains. The book is intended for use by individuals in their private meditation upon the Word, or small groups of youth and adults may find it helpful as a text for a shared study of the selected Bible passages. A guide for its use in such a study group appears as an appendix.

To help Christian men and women to know the Lord Jesus just a little bit better, that they may "see him more clearly, love him more dearly, follow him more nearly"—this is the intention and purpose of this little book.

Finally and briefly, a word of sincere thanks: to the editors of *The Lutheran* magazine, in which most of the "people stories" originally appeared; to the people of Christ's Lutheran Church, Woodstock, New York, for their understanding and support of their pastor's writing ministry.

Walter A. Kortrey

Woodstock, N.Y.
The Epiphany of Our Lord
1974

Who Is Jesus?

THE SON OF GOD
SAVIOR OF THE WORLD
WHO IS JESUS? the WORD MADE FLESH
SWEET LORD BEAUTIFUL SAVIOR KING OF CREATION?
A PLASTIC LAMP AT WOOLWORTH'S, 25 WATTS BEHIND HIS EYES— MAKE IT 40 AND HE SHEDS MORE
LIGHT!
FIRST CENTURY HIPPIE WHO FREAKED OUT ON GOD.
WHO IS JESUS?
HE WALKS WITH ME AND HE TALKS WITH ME AND HE TELLS ME I AM HIS OWN!
GOD'S ONLY SON, OUR LORD, CONCEIVED BY THE HOLY GHOST, BORN OF THE VIRGIN MARY ...CRUCIFIED, DEAD AND BURIED. ON THE THIRD DAY, HE ROSE AGAIN!
THE GOOD SHEPHERD
RADICAL REVOLUTIONARY GETTING HIS DEATH WISH.
SUPERSTAR!!!

To Know the Lord

Everyone knows him and no one knows him. Who is Jesus? Savior? Superstar? Super Myth? What was he really like, this God-man on Capernaum's fishing dock, this Teacher of the Galilean road and the Bethany apartment—what was he really like?

A true-to-life picture of Jesus is not easily arrived at. For one thing, the portraits that have come down to us through the years are all overlaid with theological distortion, superfluous sentimentality, and the thin lacquer of popular appeal. As one writer puts it, "Fundamentalist, revolutionary, ecclesiastical bureaucrat, counterculture hippie, porno film maker—all are busily engaged in making Jesus into their own image and likeness."[*] What we see so many times is not Jesus as he was and is but a composite picture of what men would have him be.

The truth is, we all see him through our own eyes, through our own lives, through our own needs, and inevitably we make him over into the kind of Jesus we want, a Lord who fits into our scheme of things.

But if a Christian is serious about his quest for the true Christ, if he has genuinely and in all good faith engaged himself in the personal struggle for Christ-likeness, then a necessary part of his devotional discipline must be to study the Gospels and to search the Word of God and to use all his powers of intellect and imagination in a determined effort to find the real Jesus. We must come to know him as a three-dimensional human being, flesh and blood and bone. Person to person, we must come to see him as one who was in every way like us, yet without sin.

It is not important to know what Jesus looked like—the color of his eyes, the texture of his skin, the cut of his beard, the true length of his hair. His photograph, if there were such a thing, would prove nothing and save no one. We need to know how Jesus looked at life and at other people. His casual conversation may be as important to us as his Gospel sermons. We need to know how he dealt with the drab and the drudge of the daily routine. The way he acted in sudden crises, his sense of humor, his temper—all these can help us to come closer to the reality of his personality, his true character.

---

[*] Andrew Greely, "A Christmas Biography," *The New York Times Magazine*, Dec. 23, 1973, p. 8. © 1973 by The New York Times Company. Reprinted by permission.

The Context of History

But where is the record of such things to be found?

> The New Testament can be treated neither as legend nor scientific history. It is not all fabrication, but it is not a journalistic account. No scholar doubts that Jesus actually existed, that he preached, that he had followers and that he was executed by the Romans. Yet, we do not know what he looked like, we do not know exactly what year he was born. We know almost nothing about his family life. It seems safe to assume that he began preaching in the wake of a powerful religious experience. But we do not know what he did before that—his friends, his interests, his education, if any . . . but because we do not know his height, or his weight, or the house in which he lived or who his childhood friends were, it does not follow that we are ignorant about him. *We can put him into a historical context, see what he was in that context and recapture the essence of his message out of that context.**

Our search for the real Jesus advances immeasurably when we study the Gospels in the context of his own time and culture. It is important to know, for example, the political climate, the power structures in Jerusalem and Palestine, prevailing economic conditions. But of greater importance, perhaps, are those insignificant threads of custom and circumstance which together became the stuff of life as Jesus knew and lived it. Such things as family customs and taboos, community events, levels of education, the place of women, current superstitions, and popular fads and fears. As we work to become, more and more, participants in the scene that was contemporary with Jesus, we begin to see new dimensions in his character and personality. Some of his familiar words, recorded in the Gospels and memorized for generations, take on new meaning. His actions and reactions in certain circumstances gain new significance and, in some cases, make more sense.

The People Person

Who is Jesus? Clearer answers to that question can come out of a careful study of his words and works in the context of his own

---
* Ibid.

time, and particularly in *the context of the people around him.* As we become better acquainted with those who lived beside him, who sought him out, whose lives were turned around by what he said and did, we will come closer to him and to the truth that was in him.

It is in the context of people that Jesus may best be known—the men and women and children who clustered around him, on the streets of Jerusalem, on the shore front in Galilee, on the road north to Sidon and to Rome. Jesus was a "people person." His whole life and ministry were spent in seeking and being sought by people of all kinds. It is true that sometimes he craved moments of solitude and the refreshment of a silent hour alone with God. "Very early the next morning, long before daylight . . . he went out of town to a lonely place where he prayed (Mark 1:35)." But his times alone were meant only for the Spirit's enabling him to return to the waiting multitudes again. And after a while, people were so drawn to him and felt such a need of him that it became nearly impossible for him to elude them.

The Gospels are filled with stories of Jesus' encounters with people: young and old, wise and simple, rich and poor, educated and uneducated, the high and the lowly, the sick and the well, the happy and the sorrowing. Day after day "the multitudes came to him" and "all manner of people were brought to him" and "the common people heard him gladly." A study of Jesus in the context of the people around him can provide fascinating insights and information which are not immediately apparent in a mere review of his words or of the notable events of his life and ministry. In an analysis of those who walked and talked with him, noting how they acted and reacted to his presence among them, we may learn new lessons about the Way of Christ, the Truth that was in him, and the Life he brought from God.

In the pages that follow, a small number of the people around Jesus have been singled out for special attention. Their relationships with the Lord, the events through which they passed with him and his transforming effect upon them, reveal in each instance some specific facet of the Master's life and personality. Before turning to these individual stories, however, it may prove helpful to set the stage with some general observations about Jesus and his impact upon all those who came under his influence.

In Their Sandals

To begin with, Jesus' deep sense of empathy was apparent in every relationship. "He knows how I feel." The rejected children, the grieving parents, the lonely old widow, the suspicious Pharisee, the despised politician, the thief on the cross—all the people around Jesus felt his sensitivity to their special circumstances, their private longings, their individual needs. He seemed, in some mystical way, to have walked in all these various sandals. All these wounds, it seemed, he had felt in his own flesh. All these hot tears had burned in his eyes. When Jesus said, "I understand," the people around him knew that he did indeed feel what they felt and that he sensed their real needs before they could themselves identify them. All the people around Jesus testify to his empathy.

The Worth of One

And they all noted his respect for their personhood. Though he could feel their need and was usually able to supply it, Jesus never imposed his will upon others. In every relationship, the Lord sought to preserve the integrity and the independence of the person before him. Riffle through the pages of the Gospel stories and see how frequently you find Jesus insisting upon individual decision making. "What do *you* want me to do for you?"—"Who are *you* looking for?"—"Who do *you* say I am?" Jesus showed a deep respect for the personhood of every man, woman, and child who ever came to him. He saw them all, not as eventual disciples, not as prospective Christians, but as children of God, each one, whom he had come to serve and save.

The Cup of Truth

Another characteristic which is seen in Jesus in nearly every relationship was his absolute demand for truth and honesty without fear or favor. He would not compromise himself or his mission for anyone. He was as open and direct with the influential Pharisee as with the derelict beggar. Even his mother had to learn this hard fact of Jesus' life. He had come to seek and to save the lost—to bring sinners to repentance. And neither the threats of his foes nor the well-meant compromises of his friends could divert him from the task that was set before him. "The cup which the Father has given me—shall I not drink it?" Resolute, determined, unflinching, his eyes and his heart were fixed upon God's truth and the fulfillment of his will.

The Lord of Love

Finally, all the people around Jesus soon became aware of the immense capacity for love that was in him. He cared. You only had to be with him for a short time and you knew; he cared. Love kept him going through the long days of healing and preaching. Love sustained him when the clouds gathered and the crowds dispersed. Love was in his serving hands in the upper room. Love anguished in Gethsemane and kept silent beneath the lash. Love suffered on the cross, and love emerged victorious on the resurrection morning. In his patience and kindness, in his gentle firmness, in his simple humility, in his giving of himself without let, Jesus made love come alive for all the people around him.

Witnesses Unaware

He left no written record of his own philosophy of life, no diary of his own activity. The real Jesus is known today through the witness of those among whom he lived and worked, suffered and died, those to whom he showed himself after the resurrection. Much of this witness in the New Testament is the direct testimony of some of the more prominent leaders of the early church, the well-known people around Jesus—Peter, John, James the brother of the Lord, the evangelists, Matthew, Mark, and Luke—and later the missionary apostle, Paul.

But the New Testament also provides another witness—the impressions and reactions of many anonymous disciples and passers-by who appear only briefly on the Gospel stage. Often overlooked, the experiences of these bit players; but their testimony between the lines, examined in the context of the New Testament message and in that historical setting, can provide new insights for the Christian in his quest for the real Jesus.

With "sanctified imagination" filling in the details, the experiences of some of the little-known and seldom-mentioned people around Jesus can be brought to life, offering significant learning experiences to the twentieth-century believer. The unknown disciple of Bethphage, the woman of Canaan, the boy with his lunch, the Cyrenean crossbearer—these and others like them are given special attention in this study. All of them show how every one of the people around Jesus has a vital role to play in the full revealing of his character and personality.

We Are His Witnesses

The people around Jesus in the Gospels—the great and the small, the known and the unknown—all serve to bring to light different aspects of his life and character. Becoming acquainted with them and noting the change which the Lord made in their lives may give us new understanding of the way he can work in us, and we can discover our own identity as the "people around Jesus" today.

Yes. In the communities in which we Christians work and play and live and love today, even as in Galilee long ago, the world of men comes to know the real Jesus especially through those who have made him the center of their lives. Now, as then, the Lord is known not by the company he keeps but by his effect upon that company—by his effect upon us. We are his witnesses as we display, in our words and actions, some small portion of his love, some faint reflection of his light.

This, then, is the purpose of this brief study—to come to know Jesus through the people around him in the Gospels and, inspired by their example, to offer ourselves as the here-and-now witnesses of his grace and glory.

Outer-circle Disciples

Followers at a Distance

The Good News does not give equal time to each of the twelve apostles. Some of Jesus' best friends are hardly mentioned. A few are listed by name and hometown, and that is the end of it. Others, unnamed, appear on the Gospel stage for a moment or two, play their part, and are never seen or heard from again. A half-dozen leading lights manage to remain front and center through nearly all the action, but except for Simon Peter and James and John, the sons of thunder, their voices are seldom heard, and, when all is said and done, we really know very little about who they were or what they were like.

It is important for the modern Christian to learn as much as he can about these low-profile disciples. Some of them, like John the Baptist, played an important part in the anticipation of Jesus' ministry and the preparation for it. Others, like Andrew, were chosen and set apart by the Lord himself. He saw some special grace, some secret strength, some hidden gift in them, and eventually they became the foundation stones of his church on earth. Finally, there were those who became friends of Jesus in a sudden encounter, responding to his call of the moment, supplying an immediately pressing need, answering an urgent cry for help.

All these outer-circle disciples have this one thing in common—their place in the Gospel story could not have been taken by another. Each was the man of the hour. Their response of discipleship was crucial, and, though we know so little about them, each one of them is significant as the one and only disciple for that one and only moment.

Among all the people around Jesus, these followers at a distance are important examples for us in our present-day discipleship. They hold up before us the great idea that there is a special place and a nontransferable role for each one of us in the Master's kingdom work. There is a job that only you can fill. There is a word that only you can speak to a soul who will not listen except to you. There is a mission and a ministry which is uniquely yours, and if you will not do it, it will not be done.

Little known, seldom heard, often anonymous, the outer-circle disciples can lead us to new truths about the Lord Jesus. They are very important people around Jesus.

The Quiet One

"Andrew found his brother Simon and told him, 'We have found the Messiah.' "
John 1:15-42
John 6:6-13
John 12:21-26

Nets and boats, hard work, and the sea wind were second nature to him. A fisherman by trade and heritage, he had lived his whole life there in Bethsaida-by-the-Sea. But strangely, he seemed not to be where he was meant to be. Not that he complained or said very much about it. He never said much about anything. But out on the sea at dawn, his eyes were often fixed upon the far horizon. He seemed ever to be seeking something more—something more. In his own quiet way he was searching for God's answer, for God's Word. He was searching for God.

That is why they finally let him take the time off to follow his own strange dream. "Let him get it out of his system," his father said. "He'll be back when the vision fades—or his money runs out!" His big, brawling brother thought him a drifter and mistook his quiet way for weakness. But his mother, watching him go, knew that he would never return to the nets and the boats and his father's trade. She knew that he would seek till he had found. That was the way it had always been with Andrew.

So the second son of Jonas went off in search of himself and his God. His quest led him first to John, that strange wilderness man. The Baptist's call for repentance and a changed heart appealed to Andrew. The life of rigorous discipline and quiet contemplation fits his nature perfectly. And there was one thing more. John spoke repeatedly of a promise soon to be kept. He looked for a new day about to dawn. "Someone is coming," the Baptist said, "who is greater than I am. He existed before I was born, and I am not good enough even to untie his sandals." Andrew could not understand all that, but somehow he knew that a stupendous God-event was in the making.

Waiting and Watching

So when Jesus came to Bethany on the east side of the Jordan, Andrew was there, waiting and watching. When Jesus walked with John into the water to be baptized, Andrew was there. And the silent son of Jonas was one of the first and one of the few to perceive the meaning and the wonder of John's words, "Here is the Lamb of God who takes away the sins of the world."

After that it seemed a natural thing that, more and more, Andrew would leave John to follow, at a distance, in the footsteps of Jesus. At last one day the Lord turned and asked his searching question: "What are you looking for?" Andrew's reply was more profound than it first seems. "Where do you live, Rabbi?" he asked. Or, more accurately: "Where do you stand, Master? What do you stand for? Where are you, Lord, in the whole scheme of things?"

There was a long silence. Then Jesus looked into the eyes and into the heart of this quiet Galilean fisherman and uttered his first call to apostleship: "Andrew, come and see!"

That was about four o'clock in the afternoon. Andrew went with Jesus and spent the rest of that day with him—only a few short hours, but apparently it was enough. By the time the sun had risen on the next morning he had made up his mind. His destiny was to follow the Nazarene, and he could already see the part in service which he must play.

Bringing Someone to Jesus

Not much is said about Andrew in the written record of the Good News, but wherever he appears, he comes, a quiet evangelist, bringing someone to Jesus: the boy with his lunch—rolls and some fish—before the feeding miracle; the inquiring Greeks ("We would see Jesus!") in those last dark days before the final week; and above all and before anyone else, his own big brother. The Good News says, "At once Andrew found his brother Simon and told him, 'We have found the Messiah [the Christ of God].' Then he brought Simon to Jesus."

Read between those lines and you will understand more clearly why Jesus called him to apostleship first, before all the others. When he was persuaded that Jesus was the very Christ who had brought God's answer to life and death, Andrew's first move was to find his brother and bring him to the Lord. That may not seem so unusual at first, but remember, Andrew had always lived in Simon's shadow. People found it difficult to remember Andrew; his name always escaped them and they usually ended up introducing him as "Simon's brother—the quiet one." From childhood and youth and into manhood, always and in everything Simon would "take over." At home with their parents, in their boyhood games, working aboard ship, with girls, Andrew always had to stand back behind his big-shot brother.

Discipleship of Standing By

So you see, Jesus' call to discipleship could have been Andrew's opportunity to come out of Simon's shadow and make his own mark, be his own man, do his own thing. He could have kept Jesus to himself. But the genuineness of his faith in Christ and the depth of his love for his brother would not permit that. He remembered the words of his first teacher, John: "Jesus must become more important, while I become less important."

Taking his cue from John, Andrew from the beginning chose the quiet discipleship of standing by, listening to the Master's voice, and finding happiness in leading the way for others. Andrew, the second son of Jonas, never had much to say. But miracles happened; lives were changed; big brother Simon became Peter the Rock and souls were saved because the quiet one said, "I have found the Christ! Come and see!"

Needed: Quiet Evangelists

The life of Andrew, the first apostle, offers insight and inspiration for the church today in its witnessing for Christ. We need his reminder that the real key to an effective program of evangelism is the faithful, committed Christian who hears the Word of God and in a quiet, selfless way invites his brother to "Come and see!" Modern methods and media must be used, but in the long run miracles happen, lives are changed, and souls are saved when one heart reaches out to another, saying, "I have found the Christ!"

Then, too, Andrew reminds us that there are, still today, in churches large and small across the world, many serving saints standing by, listening to the Master's voice; and the church's secret strength in many places is the positive witness of these self-effacing quiet ones: "I have found the Christ. Come and see!"

John the Baptist

"Tell John what you have seen and heard: the blind can see, the lame can walk, . . . Good News is preached to the poor."

John 1:19-32
John 3:22-27
Luke 7:18-28

He was a wide-sky man, this John, the one they called the Baptist. He preferred the stars overhead to a timbered roof, the green moss of the woodland to the downy ease of a house in town. The wide vistas of creation were his delight by night and day. The silent mountains, the mysterious desert, the moving river, the open field—among these he lived, and among these he became a dedicated man of God.

He sought after holiness as others seek riches. He delighted in God as other men delight in women or in wine. Heart, soul, mind, and strength he gave to his task. He knew that he was called to a holy calling, set apart for a sacred mission, and in fulfillment of it he surrendered everything.

John the Baptist was a man for all outdoors. The wind of the sea was in his nostrils, the scent of the piney woods was in his hair—and the burning flame of God's Spirit was in his heart.

Cramped by a Cell

Little wonder, then, that languishing in the dark cell of Herod's fortress, he began to wonder. Far from the sight of sun and stars, the hum of the bees, the feel of the cool earth between his toes, John—even John—began to doubt and fear. Had his zeal been all in vain? Had he dedicated himself to a false messiah? Had his devotion been betrayed? The walls of the cell seemed to close in upon him. The stale air polluted his lungs. He longed to see the eagle flying free; he yearned to hear the whispering trees—and a word, just a word, from the God who had called him.

"Are you the one, or do we look for another? Jesus, tell me true. Are you Emmanuel, the Son of God, the Savior of the World? Are you the Messiah?"

Awaiting an Answer

Undoubtedly the Christ was touched to the heart by the imprisoned Baptist's question. The simple genius of his reply may be deceiving at first. It may seem like no answer at all. He gave no secret word to prove his Lordship, no mystic sign, no lightning in a box.

Only this: "Go and tell John what you see and hear. The blind receive their sight, the lame walk, lepers are cleansed, and the deaf hear. The dead are raised up. And the poor have the gospel preached to them."

Do you see? For Jesus Christ and surely for John the Baptist, the proofs of God's presence were not to be found in theological formulas and declarations of prophetic fulfillment. "Tell John what is happening out here in the world." Then he will know that Jesus *is* the Christ. The Lord has come!

The Gospel in Action

In his dark and doubting captivity, John put this valid question to the Lord: "Are you the one—the one and only? Are you the Savior?" The simple answer was down-to-earth, practical, realistic. Show him what's happening. Works of love and mercy are being done; to all men the good news of God's love is being told. Forgiveness and peace are on his lips. Tell John that something marvelous and wonderful is happening. Show him the gospel in action.

The Same Question

We have no evidence in scripture that the witness of the Lord's ministry ever came back to comfort John, nor do we have any reference to his reaction. But, assuming that the Word was given, we may be sure that John the Baptist was satisfied and that he was ready when the cold death fell upon his neck. His mission was accomplished. His task was done, and the great question was answered.

Yes. It was answered for John. But the same question has been put to the church again and again down through the years. And when it was true to the spirit of Jesus, the church understood the need for a working Christianity. In Paul's letters you can read how he called for his flourishing congregations to share their wealth and themselves in a show of benevolence for the needs of others, near and far.

The same question confronts the church today. Is he the Savior of the present time? Does he come to redeem us in our captivity? Can he give peace, forgiveness, and lasting joy to me? Jesus! Son of God and Son of man—are you a *now* Savior? Are you the one and only lover of our souls? Or should we look elsewhere?

The Same Answer

The world is asking and the church must answer. This was Jesus' intention, after all. The church is Christ's body on earth today—his voice, his hands, his beating heart of love. And when the world asks, "Is Christ for real?" the church must reply, straight from the shoulder, as Jesus answered John, not with theological double-talk or liturgical fireworks, and not with the tangled tongues of the charismatics or the sweet fumes of pentecostal testimony either, but with the practical, down-to-earth evidence of a working Christianity—a happening gospel that cares for the sick, comforts the orphan and the widow, feeds the hungry, leads the blind, and makes love come alive in the name of Jesus.

Simon the Zealot

"News about Jesus went out through all of Judea and the surrounding territory."

Luke 6:13-16
Luke 7:17
Luke 9:51-52

Among the apostles of Jesus there were two Simons: Peter, who was nicknamed "The Rock," and then the other Simon, whom they called "The Zealot." That's all we know about him. That is the only word the Good News gives—that one word, "zealot," or, in other translations, "patriot," "enthusiast."

That one word speaks volumes. It calls forth many questions about this man and his place in Jesus' company. In the time of Christ, the Zealots were a band of revolutionary patriots who had sworn themselves to the cause of freedom for Israel and the overthrow of Roman tyranny. They were superpatriots, fanatic, violent. Much like the terrorists of today, they used the tactics of hit-and-run, the taking of hostages, threats of reprisal against fellow Jews who would not support their fanatic enterprises.

It was part of the Zealots' practice to seek, whenever they could, to tie their cause to some popular hero whether he wanted their support or not.

There can be little doubt that, when Simon the Zealot first came to Jesus, he saw the Master as the new champion of the Zealots' cause, a national redeemer.

Jesus, you may be sure, was not blind to this subversive slant to Simon's discipleship. But he called him, nevertheless, because he needed in his church the kind of zealous enthusiasm which was a natural part of Simon's character.

We have no scriptural evidence that Simon ever left the Zealots' party, but the fact that he appears as one of the apostles after the seeming defeat of Jesus on Good Friday lends credibility to the idea that Simon the Zealot, under the influence of Jesus, put down his firebrand and found a better way to channel his zeal into the constructive mission of Christian proclamation.

Repeatedly we read in the Good News such words as these: "When Jesus returned, . . . the crowd welcomed him (Luke 8:40)" or "The next day . . . a large crowd met Jesus (Luke 9:37)" and "The crowds gathered to hear him again (John 10:1, RSV)."

How did they hear of his coming? There were no newspapers with special full-page ads, no spot announcements at station-break time, not even one billboard at the side of the road to Jerusalem. We can only assume that, when the crowds gathered, someone had been busy spreading the word—"the Master is coming! The Nazarene is on his way! Drop what you're doing and come!"

Simon the Zealot, when he was converted, was undoubtedly one of the foremost of the Lord's proclaimers. He was the Master's self-appointed public relations man. Consumed with zeal for Christ, he fairly bubbled over, even when asked to keep still. "[Jesus] charged them to tell no one; but the more he charged them, the more zealously they proclaimed it (Mark 7:36, RSV)." There's that word again—"zealously." Whenever it appears in the story of Jesus, you may be sure this Simon is not very far away.

Simon the Zealot. He is one of a small company of men, rare in any age. Give them a cause and they'll take it to the moon. Their fervor is contagious. They can set fire to the lukewarm and turn casual bystanders into flag-waving adherents. They are the driving force which makes the world take note of the cause they have espoused. They are not intellectual giants, seldom named among the mighty of the earth; they are not listed in *Who's Who*. But certain things stand out.

In the first place, their zeal is genuine. They are personally persuaded, convinced in their own hearts. Their enthusiasm is not an empty show. Simon the Zealot, when he took up the Lord's cause, knocked on every door because he believed in Jesus. He advertised his Lord because he knew deep down in his own being that this carpenter with the hands of power and the eyes of grace was the best thing that had ever happened to *him*. Simon the Zealot was a man on fire, and he knew in his own way that God's Holy Spirit had kindled the flame. He was no professional drumbeater, no hollow huckster for a holy man. He proclaimed Christ because he had himself accepted Christ. So it is with all true zealots. They are themselves believers.

And then, there is another thing. On the night of Jesus' betrayal, all the disciples forsook him and fled. And Simon was one of them. But the example of zeal which he saw on the cross was enough to bring him back to his senses, back to his faith, back to his fanaticism.

Yes, fanaticism. It is one thing to be carried away by a popular hero, one to whom a crown is offered, one for whom palm branches wave and holy songs are sung. But it is quite another thing to be the proclaimer of a crucified loser. That takes a fanatic! And that is just another word for zealot. As we have noted, that word is the only record we have of this other Simon, except for the rather certain tradition that he died a martyr's death. Only a man who is personally persuaded could do that. Only a fanatic for Christ could die for his cause.

Simon the Zealot, a Christian whose zeal and raging fanaticism was converted to the cause of Christ. Does the witness of his zeal have anything to say to the church today? Yes. Simon says, "The fanaticism is missing." And it may just happen to be the quality most needed among Christians in this generation. Possibly the real key to the church's evangelism effort in any age is Simon's kind of fanatic extremism for the Lord.

And there's another word for zealot. Call it what you will, the church of Jesus Christ today is sadly lacking in zealous extremists for the good news. We don't want to stick our necks out. We are content to fit our faith into the proper forms, with the "right people" in the sheltered sanctuary. Don't ask us to demonstrate on the sidewalk for his Way of Love. That's for fanatics and, besides, it isn't safe.

Don't ask us to go from door to door as Simon did. Don't ask us to tell the man on the street, in the plane, and the train about Jesus the Savior. We're too self-conscious! Or is it that we are not really Christ-conscious anymore?

The little-known figure of Simon the Zealot in our church's history haunts us; he reminds us that the old-time religion of confinement and complacency just won't do anymore. We must be sure of our faith, and we must dare again to be Zealots for the Savior—fanatics for that dying Fanatic on the cross.

The Bethphage Disciple

"And if anyone says anything, tell him, 'The Master needs them'; and he will let them go at once."

Matthew 21:1-9
Mark 11:1-11
Luke 19:28-38

There is a hidden apostle in the Palm Sunday story, a disciple behind the scenes. We do not know his name, age, or occupation. To the best of our knowledge he never appears in person in the Gospel story. Yet his presence is unmistakably felt, and his silent hosanna puts the shouting of the multitude to shame. Go back and read this familiar passage carefully verse by verse. Think it over carefully. Can you find Palm Sunday's apostle-in-hiding?

Don't look for him up there with all the familiar names: Peter, James, and John and all the rest. They were not about to cover up their praise. They wanted to be out front where they could be seen and heard. Their glad enthusiasm was an open book for all to read that day. And we can hardly blame them. They had kept the good news shut up in their hearts for possibly three long years. Now at last it was time to break the fast of silence, to begin the feast of praise. The time had come at last to praise Jesus in the light of day and to crown him King in the sight of men. No, his apostles were not hiding.

But where is the hidden apostle then? In the crowd that gathered along the way? What a diversified group it was. Some of them no doubt remembered this pale, silent figure on the colt, remembered him from another time, another place—the Galilean seashore, the temple court, the grassy hillside out beyond Capernaum. Some of them may have eaten the bread and fish of that sacramental miracle. Perhaps a chosen few had known the mystifying wonder of his healing power on their own limbs, eyes, ears.

Surely *they* would not keep silent. Here was their opportunity to tell the world that he had come to them. "Hosanna" came readily to the lips of those whose hearts had been touched by his word, whose bodies had been healed by his hand, whose souls had been enriched by his gracious presence.

But the unseen disciple, where is he? Perhaps among the uninvolved bystanders? No. This unusual processional drew them in. Soon they left off standing by—out of curiosity, perhaps, or the need for some excitement in their lives, or just for the chance to be part of something bigger than themselves. Among these there was no silent hosanna. Indeed, after a while they shouted louder than the rest, for in reality they were calling attention to themselves and not to Christ the Lord. He was their cause célèbre for the moment. So they sang and shouted and demonstrated with greater gusto than all the rest.

A Simple Act of Love

Can you find Palm Sunday's apostle-in-hiding? It's kind of a puzzle, isn't it? But now, look at the words again: "Go to the village there ahead of you, and at once you will find a donkey tied up and her colt with her. Untie them and bring them to me."

There. Do you see? There he is. Not in the songs and the shouting, not in the frantic emotionalism of waving palms and garments in the dust. No. Much earlier, before the noise began, before the demonstrators assembled—there he is, in the opening hours of Palm Sunday, revealed in a simple, ordinary act of dutiful love. His silent hosanna is possibly the most sincere expression of praise in all that story. "Tell him, 'The Master needs them'; and he will let them go at once."

Yes. There he is. The Bethphage disciple with his praise of Christ that expressed itself in a quiet willingness to serve, adoration of the King manifested in silent dependability. The silent hosanna sings sweetly from the life of this unnamed lover of the Lord, whose love was so sincere, whose loyalty was so sure that, sight unseen, Jesus knew, "I can count on him." Just say, "The Master needs them" and at once, immediately, straightway, he will let them go.

True Praise vs. Hollow Praise

Is it too farfetched to think that Jesus the Christ was more truly praised by a jackass and its colt in their mute testimony to their master's devotion than by all the extravagant praise of the Palm Sunday multitude? As Jesus rode in silence and in private sadness, listening to the hollow praise of hollow men and weak disciples, I wonder did he, once or twice, stroke the shaggy coat of the dumb brute beneath him and feel deep in his heart of hearts a warm welling up of gratitude for the active loyalty and the doing-love of that anonymous apostle, the Bethphage disciple?

It all comes down to this. True praise of Christ the King is not expressed in lofty words and high-flown phrases. That's obvious. But not all good deeds and kind acts and church work are necessarily examples of true devotion either. Christ has had enough of our words of prayer and praise that have nothing behind them but the whistling wind. He has had quite enough, too, of the good works that we wear on our sleeves. He must be sick and tired of our flaunted service of little deeds.

Examine Your Motivations

The silent hosanna of Palm Sunday has this to teach us: the purest praise of Jesus Christ is the silent, secret deed of love, anonymously rendered and for no other purpose but to glorify the Lord, offered up for this one and only reason—gratitude to God and love of Christ the Savior, for what he is, for what he has already done.

We must learn again the lesson of the Bethphage disciple. Examine the motivations of your work for God. Is it truly service to Christ, or is there something of self-glory in it? Does it draw attention to the Lord, or does it turn a favorable spotlight on you? Is your work in any sense a salving of your conscience, a compensation for other failures that have not been resolved?

And think this one over too. Would your work of love and mercy, whatever form it takes, be as rewarding to you and would you continue in it much longer if no one but the Lord Christ knew of it?

The Bethphage disciple sang a silent hosanna on Palm Sunday. The sound of his dependability and serving love were music to the Master's ears in the midst of all that noise. Have you learned this secret song of perfect adoration? Has the Lord Jesus come to know, in thick or thin, when the whole world watches and when no one sees—can he say of you always, "I can count on him"?

The Emmaus Disciple

"On that same day two of them were going to a village named Emmaus—"
Mark 16:12-13
Luke 24:13-35

Filled with conflicting thoughts of life and death, bewildered by the incredible rumor of a resurrection, they walked together as in a waking dream, all unaware of the real world around them. Debating the bad news and the Good News, they found themselves changing sides constantly.

"If a man dies will he live again?"

"But he was *more* than a man; we always said so."

"We saw him bleed—like a man. We heard him cry—like a man. We watched him die—a man!"

"Yet today they say—he is alive! He lives!"

"It cannot be!"

"No . . . and yet . . ."

"Yes! And yet . . ."

They wanted to deny it but they could not. They wanted to believe it but they dared not. Caught in a tangle of mixed emotions, they did not hear his footsteps on the road. They hardly noticed when he overtook them on their way and fell in step beside them.

The Emmaus disciples, Cleopas and his friend, were well acquainted with Jesus. They had often heard his words of grace and glory and the coming of the kingdom. They had seen his hands of healing and compassion. At various times they had supped with him. The light of his presence had touched their lives. They should have recognized him then and there. But they did not. Though they walked with him and they talked with him, they did not *know* him.

Recognizing the Familiar

Then he opened the Word of God and began to tell them, not reading out of a book or scroll but from his inner self, "what was said about him in all the Scriptures, beginning with the books of Moses and the writings of all the prophets." There was something in his depth of understanding; "he spoke as one having authority." There was something in the mystic wonder of his voice. As they listened they had the strange feeling of having heard him just like this before, in another time, another place.

His words touched their inmost souls. Their doubts and fears subsided and they knew somehow it must be true, even as the scriptures said, that so it was ordained by God, that his Christ should come and suffer and die and rise again. They felt the fire of faith kindling in their hearts.

Yet though they were in awe of him and wondering, still they did not recognize him. But they would not let him go. When they came at last to Emmaus and home, it seemed imperative that their newfound friend should come in with them for supper. And according to their custom, they invited the guest in the house to offer thanksgiving.

See—he bows his head, this stranger, in an old, familiar way. Thus did the Lord! He holds the bread between his hands and breaks. So did Jesus hold the bread and break it!

The flame of faith burned brightly in their hearts as they watched him. Yes! It is so! See on the brow bent low in prayer? The mark of thorns is figured there! And on the hands that break our common bread—a scar! A nail's scar! He is not dead! The Lord is risen indeed!

By Word and Sacrament

It is given to but a chosen few to recognize the risen Christ with eyes of faith in one supreme, emotion-charged encounter. It happened to Mary of Magdala in the resurrection garden. Simon Peter and most of the other apostles knew the Lord at once when he came to the upper room with his word of peace. No doubt there have been others, down to this day, to whom the risen Christ came in a sudden moment of blessed recognition.

But the great majority of travelers on the road will have a conversion experience (for that is what it means to see the risen Jesus) that is more like that of the Emmaus disciples. Their eyes of faith are opened slowly but truly by the witness of the Word of God out of the holy scriptures *and* the experience of Christ's real presence in the breaking of bread in the Lord's supper.

By Word and Sacrament we come to the knowledge of the saving truth that Jesus Christ is risen from the dead. Moses and the prophets, the New Testament—the inspired scriptures reveal

God's truth and his law and his love. In them he draws near to us, and by them the fire of faith is kindled in us.

Then in the eucharist he comes to us: "My body given, my blood shed—for you!" There we are brought into God's presence. We take unto ourselves the very Christ, our Savior—crucified, dead, buried, and risen, alive, victorious—and we celebrate the communion of love which he gave to us.

And one day, with the Word burning in our hearts, and in the breaking of the bread, our eyes are opened and we know at last in faith, "It is the Lord! Our Lord is risen indeed!"

Jesus with Children and Youth

Jesus with Children and Youth

The Master had a way with children. They were drawn to him in an easy, natural way. This is seen in the Gospels more by inference than by direct report. For one thing, we know that children everywhere and in every age have loved good stories, and Jesus was a good storyteller. When he spoke to the listening crowds, he did not speak over the heads of the children. To be sure, they did not catch all the subtle shadings of meaning in his parables, but those word pictures were so clear and so full of life as they knew it that often they found themselves listening attentively and, later on, remembering and eventually grasping the deeper truth in them.

"Tell me a story!"—a timeless, universal plea of childhood. Jesus told good stories, and the little ones came to hear him again and again.

Children felt at home with Jesus. The rigid austerity and self-conscious piousness so apparent in other rabbis, and among the scribes and the Pharisees, were missing in the Nazarene. He had a gift for putting people at ease, and the children especially gathered around him. There is that pleasant vignette in the Gospel of Mark in which the contentious disciples are disputing among themselves about their comparative greatness in the coming kingdom. "He called a child and made him stand in front of them. Then he put his arms around him and said, 'Whoever in my name welcomes one of these children, welcomes me.'" How readily the child came when Jesus called. How willingly he stood before them all, knowing that Jesus stood behind him. How much at home he felt, there in the arms of the Christ.

Young children came to him, naturally, easily, confidently. And young people—adolescents, teen-agers, men and women in the springtime of life—they were attracted to Jesus too. He was a young man himself, a young man with a mission. And he let no one despise his youth. He respected his elders, fulfilled the law, and observed all the traditions of the fathers, but he gave ground to no one when he took his stand in the proclamation of the new covenant.

To some of his contemporaries, Jesus was a young radical, a rebellious youth. But to many of the young people of his day and time he brought new hope and the fulfillment at last of old promises.

The spirit of the young Jesus has great appeal to the young people of this present time, too. His call to a life of loving service comes to many young men and women. Some, like the rich young man in the Gospel story, take one step and yet another, and then, counting the cost, they turn away and he sorrows after them. Others, like Nathanael, caught up in the Christ-spirit, leave every other youthful dream behind to take up his cross and follow the Way.

The Boy with His Lunch

"There is a boy here who has five loaves of barley bread and two fish. But what good are they . . . ?"

> John 6:1-13
> Matthew 14:13-21
> Mark 6:30-44
> Luke 9:10-17

Often he had come, this boy, to watch the Master, Jesus. In the town, down by the fishing boats, and out on the rolling hills beyond, often he had come to see the power in Jesus' hands and in his eyes and to hear the lessons which he taught—lessons of God, understandable even to an eight-year-old.

Seth was one of the neighbors' children on the street where Jonas the fisherman lived. As far back as he could remember, Seth had known and idolized those two young men, the sons of Jonas. There was Simon, rough, strong, always laughing, ever playful. And there was Andrew, the silent brother. In a way, Seth liked him better. Simon was always good for a wrestling match and a hearty laugh. But Andrew was a thoughtful, teaching man. Seth found that he could sit still with Andrew for a surprisingly long time, just listening to his good thoughts, treasuring his good words.

Whenever Jesus was in the vicinity of Capernaum, Seth rejoiced. He knew that the sons of Jonas, who had left the sea to fish for men, would return, and he knew that Andrew would take him to see Jesus as often as he could. He knew that Simon would lift him high on his shoulders and carry him through the crowd to an arm's-length nearness to the Master.

But one thing bothered Seth. Often, when he heard Jesus speak, he heard him call for service: "Take up your cross—follow me—let your light shine—go and preach—comfort the fatherless and the widow—witness—feed the hungry—heal the sick—console the sorrowing." The words meant something to young Seth. He could not take them lightly. He couldn't believe that they were spoken only to grown-ups. Sometimes on his cot in the still of the night, the little eight-year-old boy would lie awake and the thought would come to him again and again: "He means me! Jesus means me. He wants me to serve. He wants me to witness. He thinks I can heal and help and do all those other things. Jesus means me!" But those words were also the cause of Seth's restlessness and troubled spirit. "What can I do? If I were Peter or Andrew, it would be different. But I'm just . . . me—too young, too little. How can I help?"

An Answer in a Bag

One day, Seth found the answer. He had come out with Simon and Andrew the day before. Oh, his mother let him; she knew he was in good hands. But good hands or no, she always gave him plenty of food to take along. He loved the little rolls she made, and the dried salted fish were for Seth what potato chips are to lots of kids today. He couldn't get enough of them.

Well, here it was the second day away from home. They had followed Jesus to the other side of the Galilean lake, and in his little homespun bag Seth had only five rolls left and two small fish. What a temptation they were! But he resisted. He knew he would be hungrier later in the day.

And then it happened. He saw the worried look on Andrew's face. And he heard Simon's loud voice: "What can *we* do? We don't have enough food for ourselves."

It was as if a chord had been struck in Seth's young brain. "What can I do?" Here was his chance! Here was the opportunity to do *something* at last. He took his rolls and his fish and he pulled at Simon's cloak. "Simon," he said, holding out his little offering, "maybe this will help."

You know what happened, don't you? Simon looked and Simon laughed. A great, big, thundering, good-natured laugh, with his head thrown back, holding both his sides. Then Seth looked at Andrew. Andrew didn't laugh. In fact, it seemed to Seth, there was a glistening tear in the corner of his eye. Silently, the quiet brother took the boy's rolls and fish and he put his hand on Seth's head and he said, "We'll see what Jesus can do with this."

"There is a boy here who has five loaves of barley bread and two fish. But what good are they for all these people?"

"Make the people sit down." The miracle happened because a little boy was waiting, waiting eagerly for a chance to serve, and when it came he was ready!

Being Ready Makes the Difference

This is the lesson that Seth learned. Not that he should be forever at Jesus' elbow with five loaves of barley bread and two salt fish. But that he should be ready. Ready to give what he had. Ready to do what he *could* do.

Seth learned that Jesus can make much of our little. He can transform our small gifts into greatness. But he *cannot* if we are not ready to offer what we have to him. Do you see? If young Seth had not been anxious, eager, restless to serve, he would never have thought to offer his gift. The impossibility of it would have stopped him cold. And the opportunity would have passed and, with it, possibly, the miracle.

Little Seth no longer need ask, "What can I do?" Now he knew. Be ready! And when the time comes, the Lord will take the gift and enlarge it and enhance it and do great and mighty things with it.

The One Thing Needful

Think about it. How many times last week could you have served the Lord but did not because you took for granted your incapacity to serve? How many miracles go undone because we do not offer up to the Master's hand the one small thing that is needful and that is ours to give?

One small deed, done unselfishly in the name and for the sake of Jesus, can by his grace beget more and more works of love, until, like the loaves and fish, they multiply and nourish souls beyond our wildest dreaming.

You can serve Jesus the Christ today, speaking his name, lifting your hand to help in some need, for no other reason but that he asks you to do so. You can witness, preach, teach, convert, and—yes, even you can heal, comfort, restore. But you've got to be ready! When the opportunity arises you've got to be on the spot and at the ready. If you hang back, if you hesitate, the moment will be lost and, with it, the miracle!

The work of teaching God's word to a needy world, of showing his love to suffering souls, of doing his will in the sight of men—this work is yours to do whenever you have the chance, with whatever you have to offer. Don't forget. However small your gift may seem to you, if it is your best, your most, Jesus will use it and he will glorify it. Just be alert, on your toes, always looking, hoping, watching for the chance to give, to speak, to act for Jesus' sake.

Be ready! "Let's see what the Lord can do with this." Who knows? Out of your humble offering of self, great things may come; miracles may be wrought and God's will may be done.

What can *I* do? Be ready. Speak, work, give when the magic moment comes, and then—leave it to the Lord.

The Rich Young Man

"With love Jesus looked straight at him and said: 'You need only one thing.' "
Mark 10:17-23
Matthew 19:16-22
Luke 18:18-23

He was what people in every age would have called "a fine young man." Clean-cut, intelligent, ambitious, responsible; he wore his hair according to approved custom; his clothes were in style but not outlandish. He carried himself with the bearing of one who was born to rule. Always respectful and courteous, especially with his elders and persons in authority, he was every inch the "perfect gentleman."

And he was rich. The clothes he wore, the rings on his fingers, the faint, fine scent of Arabian perfume gave him away. He was well heeled. But it had not gone to his head. His inner self seemed as wholesome and attractive as his outward appearance. Unlike so many rich young men, he had not been prodigal, wasting his wealth and himself in drugs and drink and sexual adventures. Jesus, looking straight into his spirit, loved him and . . . grieved over him.

Through His Own "I"

Yes. The Lord grieved over him because he could see a side of him which was not immediately apparent to others. Jesus perceived at once that the young man saw himself through his own "*I*." "What must *I* do to receive eternal life?" he asked.

"You know the commandments," Jesus answered. "Do not murder; do not commit adultery; do not steal; do not lie; do not cheat; honor your father and mother."

With the supreme and naïve self-confidence of his youth, the young man replied, "Teacher, ever since I was young I have obeyed all these commandments." Reared in a family discipline of love and obedience, with that silver spoon in his mouth, he was confident that he had done and could do anything that God or the world would ask.

"What must I do to receive eternal life?" Unlike the lawyer who on another occasion baited Jesus with a similar question, this young man was genuinely sincere in his asking. And he was absolutely certain that whatever the Lord would ask he would be able to do. The combination of wealth and a strong law-and-order life had combined to make him a kind of New Testament Lancelot. He had the moral strength, the intellectual capacity, the physical stamina; he was "blessed with an iron will"; and he had the money. It seemed an unbeatable combination, and the young man thought himself ready, willing, and able for anything.

But Jesus said, "You need only one thing." The surrender of the "I." "Sell all that you have and . . . come and follow me." The Lord was asking him to give up much more than worldly goods and gold. He was asking him to give up *himself*. "Come and follow *me*," Jesus said. "Turn your future over to me. Put your destiny in my hands. Make my will and way the determining force in your life. Sell all that you have and give yourself up for me." This is what the Lord was asking, and it was too much. It would mean a complete change of life-style, not only in material things and earthly pleasures and treasures but in his basic philosophy of life as well.

The old standard of measuring success and failure in terms of poverty or plenty would have to give way to Jesus' idea: "What shall it profit a man if he gain the whole world and lose his own soul?" The judgment of right and wrong by ritual obedience to a legal code must give way to the Christ's ideal of total grace. He would have to learn to give because he had already received so much from the Lord. He must come to love because he had been so utterly loved of God.

"Give up yourself and follow me." Too much, too much to ask. The young man found himself unequal to the Lord's demands, and he turned away, sorrowful.

The American Dream

It may seem a strange thought, but the closer I look at this rich young man, the more like a contemporary American Christian he becomes. He is the American Dream come true before its time. Highly motivated, sincere in his seeking, ambitious, smart, physically strong, mentally awake, morally straight—and, by the world's standards, a very rich young man. Supremely self-confident, he can do all things and always wins.

But Christ's idea of giving up your selfhood and your independence and all your wealth too is not consistent with this American ideal of the self-made man. As a result, we American Christians often display a kind of split image in our religious lives. We espouse a theology of justification by God's grace through faith; but in our practice we live lives of work righteousness, and we measure success or failure in the same old way —we judge right and wrong by the same old laws. And when we are confronted with Christ's demand to turn around and turn ourselves over to him and to his will, we are not up to it. We are unable to surrender the "I," and the Lord is grieved.

A fine young man came to Jesus with much to give—time and talent and treasure. "What must *I* do . . . ?" he asked the Lord.

"One thing is needful," Jesus said. "You must give yourself!"

Are *you* able?

Nathanael, the Young Apostle

"When Jesus saw Nathanael coming to him, he said about him, 'Here is a real Israelite. There is nothing false in him!' "

John 1:43-50
John 21:2
Mark 3:18

The fig tree near the well in Cana was a special place. They called it "the contemplation tree." To its shade the old men and scholar-priests came to study the writings of the fathers, to debate a point of law, to share prophetic insights, or to meditate on the meaning of life.

It was unusual to find a young man under that tree. But Nathanael and Philip were unusual young men. Their shared love of God's Word and their common hope of its fulfillment in their own time had brought them together. Beneath the contemplation tree the two had become close friends. They were both searchers, and both had been struck by the promises they found in Moses and the prophets. In and between the lines of those old books they saw the promise of spiritual renewal for the people Israel, the promise of freedom for all mankind, the promise of a deliverer come from God, the world's Savior.

The Search

Those holy promises and the hope of their fulfillment became a consuming passion for Philip and Nathanael. So it was a natural thing when the Baptist came out of the wilderness, lean, wild-eyed, fanatic, immediately the two young enthusiasts picked themselves up and followed him down to the shores of the Jordan. They sensed that somehow in him the Word was coming true—that he might even be the messiah they were seeking. But John kept saying, "No! Not me! There is someone else—someone greater, higher and more blessed. Watch for him!" After a while, the two brothers in the faith returned to the shadow of the fig tree, to study, to meditate, and to continue their search for the Living Word.

And when Jesus came, Philip saw him first and was sure. He heard his words of love and forgiveness, he saw the power of

God's compassion in him, and he was persuaded on the spot. In Jesus Philip saw all the ancient promises kept, all their searching questions answered. Philip believed, and when Jesus called, he followed.

Face to Face

But first he went to his friend under the fig tree. "We have found the one of whom Moses wrote in the book of the Law, and of whom the prophets also wrote. He is Jesus, the son of Joseph, from Nazareth." And then, knowing Nathanael—honest, forthright, openly skeptical—he made no attempt to coerce or argue an acceptance into him. He said simply, "Come and see."

Nathanael (the evangelists Matthew, Mark, and Luke all call him by his family name, Bartholomew) came then and stood face to face with Jesus. And the living Christ looked into his inmost heart and found him true, "An Israelite in whom there is no guile—there is no falsehood in him."

"How do you know me?" Nathanael asked. "How can you be so sure, so soon?"

Jesus said, "I saw you under the fig tree...."

Heart to Heart

Those words meant more to Nathanael than they mean to us when we first read them. They told him that Jesus had looked into his mind and heart. The Lord saw more than a young man in the shade of a fig tree. He saw youth in search of the truth about life. He saw youth in search of God. This Jesus was one who could confront him, not face to face, only, but heart to heart and in the deep and hidden places of his inner spirit. The Lord Jesus could see into his soul. "He knows who I am! He knows what I am seeking! He knows me! Teacher, you are the Son of God!"

Confronted with Christ

The surrender of Nathanael bar Tholmai and his subsequent call to apostleship is a Gospel event that can help the modern-day church in its understanding of its own evangelism techniques. The experience of Nathanael shows us that the only truly effective way to bring thinking men and women into the community of faith is to confront them honestly with the divine human Jesus.

They must encounter Christ. All other humanistic and moralistic "pitches," though they may be perfectly worthy and though they may in fact bring results for a time, will not change lives or command the total commitment which only the Lord, who sees into men's hearts, can inspire.

Must the church be reminded of this again? All our worship practices, traditional and contemporary; all our preaching and our teaching and all our multitude of programs, projects, retreats, workshops, cottage meetings, dialogues, family nights, coffee houses, and coffee klatches—all must have this single primary purpose above all others: that men may come to know Jesus the Christ, who knows them in their inner hearts, who cares for them as they are and calls them to follow him. "We have found him! He is the one! Nathanael . . . come and see—Jesus!"

III

The Sick and the Sorrowing

The Healing Jesus

Jesus came healing. This fact is made very clear in the Gospel of Matthew: "People brought him all those who were sick with all kinds of diseases, and afflicted with all sorts of troubles: people with demons, and epileptics and paralytics—Jesus healed them all (Matt. 4:24)."

Jesus was a healing master, and none who came believing were turned away. But, incredible as it may seem, he did not heal en masse, with a single word spoken for all the multitude of afflictions before him, or with one exorcising hand held high, a gesture of instant health for all. No. Jesus healed them one by one, coming to each person in his own pain, touching each life in its special anguish.

All those who felt the Master's healing in their bodies, minds, and spirits would testify to this—his healing miracles were not an inevitable certainty, a sure cure every time to everyone. Certain questions must be raised; individual diagnoses must be made. His approach and manner were different, depending upon the personal circumstances in each case, but, in one way or another, Jesus put three questions before all who came to him for healing.

First he asked, "What is wrong?" The one who is sick and those who seek to help him must know "where it hurts." They need to recognize the real source of the trouble. Jesus knew that many who came to him seeking relief from some ache and pain might find relief for a time but never true healing until they faced up to the hidden afflictions of the mind and the emotions which lay at the heart of their anguish. He made each one answer the question for himself: "What ails you?"

And then he asked, "What do you want me to do?" The question was offensive to many at first. It seemed so obvious that they wanted and needed relief from their pain, freedom from their anxiety. But many of them had built their lives and their lifestyles upon their affliction. Take it from them and they would be lost—with nothing to rail against, with nothing to complain about, with nothing to draw attention to themselves. Jesus knew that when you take away a man's need for crutches, he will not always thank you for it. So each afflicted one must look into the question, "What do you want me to do?"

And finally, by direct question or by his own sensitive probing of each troubled spirit, Jesus asked, "Do you believe?" Do you believe that God cares, that his caring brings healing? But do you believe that sometimes his caring brings not peace but a cross? Do you believe in God? Do you believe in me? Faith was an essential prerequisite in every one of Jesus' healing miracles. The afflicted one himself, or someone close to him, must come with these words on his lips or in his heart: "Lord, I believe that you can make me clean!"

The sick and troubled people around Jesus have much to tell us about him and his healing way. The healing ministry of the church today can benefit from their witness. Like Jesus, the church must come face to face with every suffering soul, concerned and caring about each one in his own place. And the church must ask the Master's questions: "What is wrong?" "What do you want God to do?" "Do you believe?"

Bartimaeus, the Blind Man

" 'What do you want me to do for you?' Jesus asked him."

Mark 10:46-52
Matthew 20:29-34
Luke 18:35-43

The son of Timaeus had lost his sight, but there was nothing wrong with his hearing. As a matter of fact, since the veil had come over his eyes he had given closer attention to the sounds around him. With his sharp ears and his keen mind he had learned to "see" much of what was happening in the near circle of his Jericho world. Discerning every footfall, he could tell with astonishing accuracy how many people were going by at any given moment, and he knew the distribution of men, women, and children among them. He could instantly identify ox cart, chariot, and barrow by the rumble of its wheels, and whether a man on foot was bearing a heavy burden or traveling light. Even the wealth of a man he could approximate by the rustle of his garments. After a while, the sound and timbre of voices revealed much to him about the speaker's integrity and character. And he learned how to interpret silence.

Like that morning when the Nazarene went by. Suddenly the usual street sounds stopped. Bartimaeus heard the hush and turned toward it. He knew that something special was afoot. A crowd was gathering, that was certain. But—strange!—it seemed a sabbath crowd in the middle of the week: women and children and men in murmured conversation. Straining to hear what he could not see, at last out of the muddle one word came clear: Jesus!

That name meant something to the son of Timaeus. For nearly three years he had turned it over and over in his mind. So many stories came back to him of healing and sight restored in other places, to other people. Listening, learning, hoping, he had waited for this moment. Blind though he was, he could see that at last his opportunity had come.

"When he heard that it was Jesus of Nazareth, he began to shout, 'Jesus! Son of David! Have mercy on me!' " The words of the blind man's kyrie and the crowd's response to them are significant. Bartimaeus saw Jesus as more than a miracle worker of the moment, more than a convenient answer to his immediate need. In calling Jesus "Son of David" the blind man declared his faith in Jesus the Christ, the promised Messiah, the only Savior, the Son of God. And it was precisely such a claim which the temple authorities were waiting to hear, that they might bring the charge of blasphemy against the Nazarene.

When the crowd tried to silence Bartimaeus, it was not that they wanted to keep him from Jesus or deprive him of mercy and healing. It was rather that they saw his words of faith as extremely dangerous, filled with all kinds of fearful implications. What is more, most of them had not yet come to see Jesus with Bartimaeus' eyes of faith, and they were not ready to take upon themselves the risks that such faith demands.

The Stunning Question

The more they tried to shut him up, the more he cried, "Mercy, mercy, Son of David, have mercy!" And Jesus heard his cry of faith and called for him. "Cheer up! Get up, he is calling you." Bartimaeus responded in a bounding reflex of joy—"threw off his cloak, jumped up and came to Jesus." Reaching, groping, stumbling, staggering through the crowd, he came to the Master who had called for him and—was stunned by Jesus' question: "What do you want me to do for you?"

For one fearful moment Bartimaeus wondered if Jesus too were blind. "Can he not see the staring, clouded pupils of my sightless eyes? Has he not marked the beggar's cup hanging from my waist and the groping, twisting path my footsteps make?" Bartimaeus wondered. Was this in truth Jesus the Son of David for whom he had waited, in whom he had believed, to whom he had cried? Or was he being mocked by some cruel pretender? He listened for some clue. He strained to hear the vision that his blind eyes could not see. And then the question came to him again: "What do *you* want me to do for you?"

His perceptive ears caught the strength and the promise in the voice of Jesus. His faith returned, and with it came a new understanding of God's way with men. The Master's question was not meant to mock him. It was meant to make him take the measure of his own faith. Surely Jesus knew who he was and what he needed most. But this was the Master's question: Does *Barti-*

maeus know who he is and what he surely needs? And does he believe that Jesus the Son of David can give it? "What do you want me to do for you?"

The blind man's answer was not so much a prayer as it was a creed. "Teacher, I want to see again!" Implicit in that petition is this article of faith: I believe you are the Christ of God who can open my eyes and save my soul.

There is a sense in which we all come to Jesus as men who have lost their sight. Stabbing in the dark, feeling our way, struggling and straining to see the light. The Gospel story of Bartimaeus the blind man tells that faith alone in Jesus the Son of David can open our eyes. And such eye-opening faith has two marks upon it: tenacity and perception.

Yes, tenacity. Saving faith, the kind that restores our sight, does not give up easily. It calls to God in an unceasing kyrie. Lord have mercy. Lord have mercy. Lord have mercy. It will not be silenced, for it knows that in his time the Lord will come. "Cheer up! Get up, he is calling you."

Then, perception. Faith that heals and saves is a faith that takes the measure of itself and perceives what is real and what is not. It can distinguish a need from a desire. It can tell the difference between an impossible dream and the Blessed Hope in Christ.

And it knows how to answer the Lord when he asks, "What do *you* want me to do for you?"

The Centurion and His Servant

"Just give the order and my servant will get well."

Matthew 8:5-13
Luke 7:1-10
Mark 15:39

The young man's memory of that day and those hours was like a battle-scarred banner, torn and tattered, with great gaping holes and so much missing. He remembered it was just past noon when suddenly the fever came upon him: a dizziness and a falling, down and down and dark and darker as into Vesuvius. After that there were only scattered moments of light and sound and recognition, all out of touch with time—a voice calling and caring, his master's face, a brittle gray mask, and the young medicus from the barracks, confused and anxious. Then again a darkness and the fever, like a shrinking helmet closing tighter about his brain.

He could not remember how long he lay there at death's door. He knew only that at last there appeared in the darkness a pinpoint of light, that it grew in size and intensity as it descended upon him like the tip of a burning lance. He tried to struggle out of its path but could not. Suddenly there was a piercing and a burning and then the breath of a cool wind on his brow and, within and all around him, a healing.

The Master's Return

They brought him then a tea of herbs with a mixture of joy and bewilderment, for none could tell what strange power had delivered him. He was already up and about and at his customary chores when, toward evening, the master returned. He stood in the doorway, a strange, knowing smile upon his lips, but he made no reply as they told him of his aide's mysterious recovery.

Later that night, made bold by the wonder he had passed through and all the mysterious things that were being said about it, the servant went to his master. Standing there in the lantern light, feeling his courage fading and stammering, he asked, "Will you tell me, sir? See? I am well again—what—how?" For a long time there was no reply. The servant feared that his master might turn on him in anger.

Faith in the Law

The young man had served the centurion as valet and aide for more than seven years, first in bondage, then as a free man. His master, commander of the Second Century (one hundred men) in the Third Legion of the Army of Rome in Palestine, had come up through the ranks and earned his place by constant and disciplined devotion to duty, unflinching allegiance to the Code of Caesar, and absolute trust in his superiors. The centurion felt at home among the Jews because he saw them as a people of faith in the law. Were it not for the stigma that it might bring upon the legion, he could easily have become a Jewish proselyte. His "religion" was already the practice of a disciplined devotion to the law in which he trusted.

The servant recalled his liberation—the day he received his freedom papers. There was no great show of emotion, no talk of "devoted servant" and "loving master." The commander had only said, "I think you are ready, my son. Go find a master you can trust; give yourself to him in everything. In faithful obedience you will discover true and lasting freedom."

And the young man replied, "I have found such a master. I trust your word. Serving you, I am already free."

The two never spoke of it again. But a new spark of equality and mutual respect was struck in that moment and remained with them.

New Stature

But the servant felt uneasy now—as if he were intruding on a part of the master's life in which he had no proper place. Yet he could not stifle his own curiosity. Sick unto death only hours before, now his mind was clear, his strength had completely returned. He had to know: Why? How? What strange power had delivered him?

"Tell me what happened, sir. Did the fever in my brain and body simply burn itself out? Did the medicus' poultice actually draw out the poison in my veins? The household says you found a healer out of Nazareth. Did you really go to a magician? Or did he come to you? What did he say? How did he work his miracle?"

The centurion turned then and stood face to face with his man. The thought went through the servant's mind: Roman though he is, commander though he is, I have never seen him stand so tall! And there was something else, hard to describe. It was as if the master had brought a happiness home in his hands, as if he had good news to tell and could hold back no longer.

At last he answered. "My son, I know not 'what' or 'how.' I surely know not 'why.' But I know *'who,'* and that is all that matters. At last, at last, *I* have found the Master for whom I have been searching all my days. For months now I have been watching, first at a distance, then closer and still closer. I know now. I have found a master I can trust and follow. When he gives the word—to be sure, it is as if he *is* the Word—when he commands the possessed are freed of their tormenting spirits, the blind see, the deaf hear, the wind and the sea obey him, and his word has restored you to us!"

The commander paused for a moment, breathless, as if the great thoughts he was thinking were too much to bear or tell. "They call him Jesus, the Christ," he said. "He comes out of the Jews, and worse, he is a Galilean, but he is a Master for all people for all time. I have found in him the truth and life and possibly—God! Yes, my son, I have found *my* Lord and he will make *me* free!"

The faith that astonishes even the Christ ("I have never seen such faith . . .") is the faith that does not ask what or how or even why. The faith that heals and saves and frees is the faith that simply accepts the Lord for *who* he is—God with us, the very Christ, the Living Word of truth and life.

The Ungrateful Lepers

"Weren't all ten men made clean? Where are the other nine?"
Luke 17:11-19

It's hard to believe, isn't it? How could they use Jesus so? What a shallow faith they had. He was a means to an end, no more. The real wonder is that the Lord accepted them. How quickly their hearts hardened. They were redeemed! Redeemed from a living death and they took it as their just deserving. The height of ingratitude! They exploited God's mercy! "Where are the nine?"

Don't be too hard on them. Or judge them too quickly. Yes, it is true. Their faith was shallow. They came crying to Jesus outside the city gate because they had everything to gain and nothing to lose. They believed in him because there was nothing else left to believe in. Their faith was a poor faith, born in despair, a last-resort thing. Their scabby hands were clutching at straws. But apparently it was enough for Jesus—as a first step in faith, it was enough. "Go show yourselves to the priests," he said. And because they'd leave no stone unturned, because they couldn't take the chance of missing any opportunity, they trusted him and took the road to Jerusalem. Don't wag your head and think too poorly of them. You know how it is, don't you?

Do you call for Christ at the top of your voice when your hands are steady and your flesh is firm? Do you? When your moneybag is full and your wife is singing in the kitchen or your husband is whistling in the garden and your children are playing around your legs, happy and gay, safe and sound—is that when you fall to your knees, believing and hoping against hope that God is true?

No. Most of us are too much like the nine ungrateful lepers, more apt to call to Christ when the mysterious spots appear—and spread. When the bones ache and the heart falters. When the singing stops and the smiles fade—and they cast you out beyond the wall—unclean, unclean. That's when we're ready to try anything, to believe in anyone. Even Jesus of Nazareth. Isn't it true? Astonishing the faith we have when all else fails. Remarkable how we can pray when prayer is all that's left. You know how it is. So don't be unfair with them.

Yes, it's true. They never came back. And such ingratitude seems incredible. But put yourself in their sandals. One moment they were on the road to Jerusalem, walking corpses. Then suddenly they were alive once more, not zombies.

I don't know about you, but I think if something like this happened to me, in all honesty, my first thought would be to get back to my wife and kids. I'd want to hold them in my arms again and tell them they wouldn't have to beg anymore, or weep, or go without. The breadwinner is home! I'd want them to touch my clean skin. I'd want to see the fear go out of their eyes, to see the smiles return. And I'd want to get back to my shop and my tools and my second chance. Wouldn't you?

You know, I have an idea that when the healing came, none of them even stopped to say good-bye to each other. And they had become very close friends in their misery. Oh, maybe one or two of them waved, but there was nothing more than that. They all rushed clean back into their own lives.

I think they meant to say thanks to Jesus. Surely it passed through their minds. But to go back would have taken them out of their way. Their homes and their loves were on another road. So they put it off. They put him off. And they said to themselves, "We'll find him this weekend. And introduce him to the family. Or maybe he'll come to our village, and we won't even have to stop working!"

You can understand, can't you? Have you ever had a reprieve like theirs? When it came, what did you do? What do you think you'd do? Most of us are just like the nine of them. They didn't run to Jesus, and neither do we. They rushed headlong back into their lives—back to the kisses, back to the gold, back to the world —and so do we.

So don't be too hard on them. If only Christ had been there when the healing happened, maybe things would have been different. But he wasn't. He didn't touch their sores the way he touched the blind man's eyes or the cripple's twisted limbs. He wasn't anywhere around when the running pus dried up and the scales fell off and the sound flesh knit itself around their bones again. He wasn't anywhere around.

So how could they be so sure that *he* had done it? After all, his was not the only healing they had sought. It could have been that Arabian mystic who showered them with rose dust only the week before. When he took their money, he told them it might take a while. It might have been that hawk's-egg ointment they bought from the old hag up in the hills. Or maybe it was that green pool they had bathed in, in Samaria. How could they be sure that Christ was their healer? They didn't *see* him do it. If only he had been there when it happened. *The farther away they got from Jesus, the harder it was to believe that he was their healer.*

We know how it is, don't we? We're not much different from the nine of them. We pray for deliverance from pain, from trouble, from death. But so often, when the deliverance comes, our astonishment at its appearance betrays our initial doubt. And when we are redeemed on a later day, at an unexpected hour, in a way we had not imagined, we find it difficult, sometimes embarrassing, to say that it was God's doing. We rummage through our lives to find other reasons: "It was my good fortune—must be doing something right!—it was my own cleverness—my self-discipline paid off at last—I finally found the right doctor—maybe it's my clear conscience!" So, the farther we get from Jesus, the easier it becomes to credit ourselves and the more difficult it is to see him as our healer.

Ten men called to Jesus out of their desperate need. And ten were healed. But only one was made *whole*. Only the Samaritan stranger moved from a feeble faith in Christ the Cure-all to a total faith in Christ the Savior.

Try not to judge the others too harshly. Try to understand. Their faith in Jesus stopped too soon. They believed in him only as a healer of this world's aches and pains—a specialist in leprosy. They saw him as the deliverer of the here and now. And so they missed the best of what he had to give. He had cleansed their bodies, but he came to cleanse their souls. He had cured their leprosy, but he yearned to cast out their sin. He had given back their lives, but he wanted to give them *life*. And they would not have it. They did not see beyond the flesh. And neither do we.

What are the loudest cries he hears from us, after all? When our hearts stretch and strain to reach him and his grace, what do they seek? "Master, have mercy! Make the tumor benign! Make the tumor benign! Master, have mercy! That pain in my chest— say it's indigestion, Lord, say it's indigestion! Master, have mercy! Restore my wayward son; keep me solvent; show us how to stop fighting. Master, have mercy!"

Think of what they lost! They were within walking distance of God's total grace, yet they turned their backs and went the other way. They did not seek the total cure, perhaps because they were not willing to confess their total corruption.

And we *are* very much like the nine of them, aren't we? The Christ who cures is ever popular with us. The Christ who heals is always welcome. What a friend we have in Jesus, the problem solver! But the Savior who would redeem our souls and take possession of us—him we would put off to another day. The Lord who can make us whole demands that we return to him and fall at his feet in total faith and in confession of our soul's leprosy. But this we are reluctant to do. Perhaps someday, but not yet. Not now.

So, in coming to Christ, we are healed for a time but never made whole for eternity. Then said Jesus, "Were not ten cleansed? Where are the other nine? Feeble in faith, forgetful of God's mercy, failing in gratitude, rejecting God's grace. Where are the nine?"

Here we are, Lord. At last!

IV

Jesus and Women

Jesus and Women

He was a boy in a typical Nazareth household, under the loving discipline of a devout Jewish mother, a first-born son enjoying the coddling maternal indulgence of all the women in the family.

He was a teen-ager struggling with adolescence and feeling deep within himself mysterious changes taking place, unfamiliar powers asserting themselves, and a new sense of his own virility and manhood.

He was an eligible bachelor with a touch of ascetic mystery about him, and his choice of the rabbinical life did not for a moment discourage the girls of Nazareth from thinking of him as a prospective husband.

When he finally set out on his mission of healing and preaching, women everywhere were drawn by his compassionate spirit, his natural way of showing that he cared, his quiet inner strength. Jesus is revealed in the Gospels, a true man in every respect, living the life of a normal Palestinian male.

There were many women in the life of Jesus. From his earliest hours, as a baby in Mary's arms, he learned about women and the many sides of a woman's nature.

The women around Jesus and his relationships with them have been variously interpreted down through the centuries. The idea of his romantic involvement with Mary Magdalene or with the other Mary in Bethany or with the unnamed woman who washed his feet with her hair has tantalized novelists and playwrights in every age. The modern Danish pornographers with their sensational film *The Loves of Jesus* are exploiting a fantasy as old as the Gospel. Such flights of fiction and fancy may be great box office, but they add nothing to a Christian's understanding of Jesus.

It is better to take the Gospel at its word. Jesus was a true man in every way, with all the instincts and desires of a true man. But because of his singular devotion to the call of God upon him, it is very unlikely that he ever considered a romantic love relationship with any woman.

He had a way to go, a work to do, a cross to bear that could not be shared with anyone. If we understand this basic premise, it will be easier for us to comprehend the many aspects of Jesus' relationships with women.

His dealings with them were always kind but firm. He was courteous always. Even the prostitute in the gutter saw herself a person in his eyes. He did not defer or condescend, even to his mother. The grieving widow, the anxious mother with her ailing child, Martha in her kitchen, Mary in her contemplation, the ambitious mother of James and John, the woman of questionable reputation—all knew the Lord to be a strong and gentle man, a compassionate lover of their souls.

The Gospel stories reviewed in the following pages show the Master in his relationships with women—sensitive to their feminine difference but respectful always of their personal independence.

Mary, His Mother

"Mary remembered all these things, and thought deeply about them."

Luke 1:26-56
Luke 2:1-21
John 2:1-12
John 19:25-27

Tucked away in a hidden corner of her heart, every mother has a secret treasure of memories, begun in her child's infancy and accumulated through the passing years. There are the usual things, like the first tooth (when it came in and when it fell out), the first steps taken, the first words spoken, and all the bittersweet departures—off to kindergarten, off to camp, off to college, off to the state of matrimony. Every mother keeps an album of joyous memory and sorrowful reflection deep within her heart.

He Was Her Baby

The mother of Jesus was no exception. "Mary remembered all these things, and thought deeply about them." She remembered the curious, suspicious strangers in Bethlehem, the crude birthing place, and Joseph's clumsy midwifery. And afterward, when the baby had come, alive and squalling in his bewildered father's arms, Mary remembered, through the semiconscious haze, the unfamiliar voices all around telling of starshine and strange music and an ancient promise fulfilled.

Mary remembered when they put her child into her arms for the first time. "All is well," they said, and Joseph was smiling now, relieved. But a mother must see for herself. Touch and test the soundness of his flesh; count the fingers, one by one, and the tiny toes. Whisper "love" into the baby ear and watch for signs of the child's hearing. Feel the breath of the new life on her breast and the silent prayer of thanksgiving beating in her heart.

Mary remembered well those early moments and the days that followed, when the temple signs of her first-born child's special grace were given in the testimony of Anna, the widow-prophetess, and in old Simeon's Benedictus—"with my own eyes I have seen your salvation (Luke 2:30)." Mary kept all these things and pondered them in her heart.

He Was Her Boy

As time went on, there was much that Mary did not understand. More and more frequently, as Jesus grew, he asked questions that went beyond a child's normal curiosity. Like any other boy, he asked about the world and how it came to be. But he seemed even more curious about himself and his own origins, about life and death and the meaning of it all. Her boy Jesus was obedient, well-mannered, in every respect a "good son in Israel." But now and again he would come in from helping in his father's shop and he would speak of his "Father's will" or his "Father's word" or his "Father's house" in a way that mystified Mary and troubled her deeply. Sometimes she felt she did not know this boy, this son of promise.

When he left home to make his own way in the world, Mary felt an emptiness and a strange, unsettled fear in her heart for him. If only he had taken up his father's trade; if only he had found a loving wife among the girls of Nazareth; if only he had settled down, nearby, in the comfort and security of their old hometown.

He Was Her Savior

It was a long time before Mary, in her heart and mind, could let him go. In the stable beneath the star she had held him close; he was her own, then, at her breast, under her wing. In the little house in Nazareth he came when she called, trimmed the lamps, brought the water, kept the fire, and was "subject unto her." But, she remembered, he began to slip from her heart's grasp that day in the temple. He had become a man in Israel, and now he said, "I must be in my Father's house."

In that moment, Mary began to realize that her son Jesus had heard a voice she could not hear. A power was drawing him that she could not persuade him to resist. Wistfully, she remembered that day in Cana at the wedding. She had not meant to domineer, but as mothers will, she had boxed him into commitments he had not chosen for himself. "You must not tell me what to do," he said. He was her son, her first-born son, but at last it came to Mary that he had never been totally her own. Even back there in Bethlehem, he was born for others; he belonged to the world.

At last beneath the cross it all came clear, all that she had pondered in her heart from the Annunciation to Good Friday. Through her tears she could see her dying son was the living Son of God, the world's redeemer. He was her baby, he was her boy, and now at last she understood—he was *her* Savior too.

Mary stored up all her memories of Jesus—the stable baby, the son of promise, the teaching master, the crucified Lord, the risen Savior. She pondered them in her heart and at the last, as when it all began, she said, "I am the handmaid of the Lord; let it be to me according to your word (Luke 1:38, RSV)."

Mary Magdalene

"She answered, . . . 'They have taken my Lord away, and I do not know where they have put him!' . . . Jesus said to her, 'Mary!'"

Luke 8:1-3
Matthew 27:50-61
Mark 16:1-10
John 20:11-18

Her grief was more than the usual graveside sorrow. Upon the cross she had seen a promise broken—bleeding. She had witnessed the crucifixion of her own hope. She had heard love's last gasp. Now, the open door of the tomb seemed to beckon to her, and in her despair she wished that she might enter it and die.

Then he came, Jesus, alive, and stood before her in the garden. But the blur of her own tears kept her from seeing him; the sound of her own heartbreak kept her from hearing his voice through the words, "Why are you crying? Whom are you looking for?"

Long years after, trying to remember every moment of that glory morning, she recalled how she had mistaken him for a gardener or some other working man around the place. And then he called her by her name, "Mary!" When she heard the familiar accents of his love, there was a resurrection of joy in her heart and she knew it was true—the promise is kept, hope is alive, Jesus the Christ is risen indeed!

From Death into Life

"Jesus said to her, 'Mary!'" It was not the first time he had called her so. In just this way he had come—it seemed a lifetime ago—on a forgotten road somewhere beyond Magdala. For the most part, the memory of those dreadful days before her deliverance had been mercifully blotted out, but now and again in a sudden moment of recall she would remember the darkness closing in and the loss of control that sent her out into the night, alone and vulnerable. Then always there came a return of consciousness, an awakening in strange places in utter humiliation.

It was a living death. She remembered how everyone else had given up; everyone else had cast her out. She was not a leper but she had been treated like one: shunned, rejected, an object of scorn and malicious gossip. She was possessed by forces they could not understand or cope with, so they chose to blame her condition on evils that were more familiar to them. Unable to exorcise her demons, they called them by other names and thus justified their turning away from her.

But then Jesus came, caring. She could not remember how she met him or when or where. She knew only that one day, all in a moment, there were his eyes looking into hers, his hand upon her brow, and his voice calling, "Mary!" And as she came to herself, she felt not shame but a cleansing and a peace! He made no judgments, asked for no plea, guilty or not. He simply and purely loved her for her own sake, and his great heart reached out to help and heal. He respected her as a troubled child of God. *He called her by her name,* from sorrow into joy, from despair into hope, from death into life.

The First Eyewitness

Mary Magdalene was the first to see the risen Jesus. Oh, at first her own tears shut him out; self-pity was as a veil over her eyes. But then he called her by her name, and the love that had healed her broken life and dispossessed her demons opened her eyes to the glory of his resurrection victory.

Love Power

Mary Magdalene found in Jesus the meaning of true love: all-giving, all-enduring, an unfailing tenderness. Mary learned from Jesus the unique dimensions of God's love, embracing all the world but calling each one by name. It is eternal, "as it was in the beginning, and ever shall be," but it is here and now.

And Mary learned this too—that love is the hidden spark of God's almighty power. She knew that all that he had done for her and in her had the energy of love behind it. It was his love that sought her, love that brought her out to freedom and clarity. His selfless, all-giving love restored her personhood; love had brought life out of death there in Joseph's garden.

God Knows Your Name

This is the word and the witness of Mary Magdalene to us in our struggle with life and our seeking after God. He knows your name. There is no one so low but that he will reach down. There is no one so lost but that he will find. There is no one so demon-ridden but that God in his Christ-love will come and redeem.

God loves you as you are. And his love can change things and make them new. Mary would say, "Look what he did for me!" God's love has the power to turn your sorrow into joy. He can bring hope into your corner of despair; and when he calls you by your name on the resurrection morning, you will see with your own eyes that Christ is risen indeed and his love has brought life out of death to you.

Salome, the Mother of James and John

"Then the mother of Zebedee's sons came to Jesus with her sons, bowed before him, and asked him for a favor."

Matthew 4:21
Mark 15:40
John 19:25
Matthew 20:20-28
Matthew 27:56

She was a Jewish momma. She wanted only the best for her boys and, as all mothers will, she sometimes took things into her own hands. They never would have had their own boat and their own place in the Capernaum market if she had not insisted. Her husband, Zebedee, was content with the good life of a simple Galilean fisherman. He thought he could want nothing better for his sons. But his wife was ambitious for them. They must have not a boat but a fleet of boats. They must be not simply fishermen but the founders of a fishing dynasty. When it came to James and John, Salome would settle for nothing but the very best.

That is why it was such a disappointment when they took off without warning. They didn't even come to talk it over with her, just dropped everything to follow Mary's oldest boy, that strange one, Jesus. Oh, he was her nephew and Salome didn't want to hurt Mary's feelings or cause trouble in the family, so she tried to keep her mouth shut. But she couldn't understand how her sister put up with him—his long silences even when he was a boy, his wanderings up in the hills, his constant questioning. When he went away, off into the desert, Salome was relieved, to tell the truth, and soon she forgot all about him. But then he returned, an itinerant rabbi and a miracle worker, and Salome was dismayed to see how her sons immediately were drawn to him. Impulsive as they always were, out of a clear sky one day they turned their backs on the fishing trade and threw in their lot with Jesus.

Zebedee only wagged his head and tried to philosophize. "They are still fishermen, of a kind," he said. But Salome felt a deep hurt and a rejection. "After everything we did for them!" she lamented.

But the time passed and things changed and you can't keep a good Jewish momma down. Soon the news began to filter back to Zebedee and his wife about Jesus' growing popularity among the people. "The whole world is going after him," they said. Salome's pride in her sons returned as she heard their names mentioned too. They had become leaders among Jesus' men. They had taken charge—the "sons of thunder." Salome liked the sound of that, and little by little she found a new dream building in her heart for her boys.

The kingdom of David was coming again! A new nation was soon to rise! And her James and her John could be cabinet officers at the very least—if they would only push themselves a little! "You won't get anywhere if you don't ask! Look at Simon! He's always making noise, talking big, and already he thinks he's boss! Don't wait until everything's settled. Tell Jesus what you want. After all, you're his own cousins! Go to him today! Tomorrow at the latest! If you don't, I'll go myself!"

James and John knew where their thunder came from, and some of the lightning too! And they did what their mother told them to do.

The record in the Good News tells this story in two ways. In Matthew's account, the mother of Zebedee's sons makes the first move and speaks to Jesus herself while her boys stand sheepishly alongside. In Mark's version, the two men come to the Master on their own, without their mother. However the request was made, of this we may be sure—Momma's pushing power had a lot to do with it.

"Promise that these two sons of mine will sit at your right and at your left when you are king."

"You don't know what you're asking. . . ."

No. She did not know. Salome did not, at that moment, understand the implications of her request, nor did her sons. Jesus was on his way to be a king, that is true, and he had come to put a new law in men's hearts. But his law was love and his way to the throne was to be a path of painful humiliation, suffering, and self-sacrifice. To follow him and to sit at his side would bring no gold, no glory in the sight of men, but a casting out, a bitter rejection, and eventually, perhaps, a martyr's death. These were not the jewels which Salome sought for her sons. She did not know what she was asking.

And she did not really understand what the Lord meant when he said, "If one of you wants to be great, he must be the servant of the rest; and if one of you wants to be first, he must be your slave—like the Son of Man, who did not come to be served, but to serve and to give his life to redeem many people."

The marks of greatness in the kingdom of Jesus are servitude, humility, the contrite heart, the spirit of love that turns the other cheek and goes the second mile. But Salome did not understand —until she stood beneath the cross. There it all came clear at last.

Watching and waiting, her heart breaking for Mary, she heard the words, "Father, forgive," she saw the Saviors total sacrifice, and the blessed truth—the marvelous paradox of the Christian life—opened up to her: To be alive to God, you must die to self, and the glory of the Christian life is in the love it gives away.

Martha of Bethany

"He came to a certain village where a woman named Martha welcomed him in in her home."

Luke 10:38-42
John 11:17-27
John 12:1-7

When you passed through the doorway of the old house in Bethany, you entered Martha's world. She knew little and cared less about the rise and fall of time and life beyond those friendly, familiar walls. Nearly all her years had been spent beneath that roof. There at that hearth Martha knew who she was, and there she was content. She felt at home in her apron and happy in her housework. Making beds, baking bread, trimming lamps, bringing water from the well, sweeping floors, washing clothes, getting ready for company—Martha delighted in all these common tasks. She felt especially called and especially gifted to make a house a home.

So down through the years, though Lazarus and Mary had always lived there too, in that Bethany neighborhood, the little cottage came to be known as "Martha's place," and very early in his ministry Jesus discovered the faith and the friendship that would always wait upon him there.

The Lord's Housekeeper

In her little place in Bethany Martha became the Lord's housekeeper. Some women have a sixth sense about the care and feeding of a man, and Martha was one of them. She saw and served the needs of the human Jesus as only her kind of woman could. She knew when he was tired by the look in his eyes and the sigh when he sat down in his favorite chair. She could tell when he was hungry. She knew when to distract him and ease his mind with small talk about the new buds in her garden or the cloak she was weaving for Lazarus. She had the rare insight to know when to leave him alone, with his feet up. In her special way, Martha made a home for the man Jesus, possibly the only real home he knew through those turbulent years of his preaching ministry.

A Service of Simplicity

Martha's discipleship was a serving of the Lord's humanity. With her brother and sister, Martha had come to a deep and abiding faith in Jesus the Christ. Her life had been changed by his friendship. To be sure, there was much that she did not understand about him and his way, but it was not in her to press and probe. Sometimes, in the stillness, she sensed that she had not yet uncovered the whole truth and wonder of the Word in him. She had questions about life and death that must one day be answered, but for now it was enough to wait on him and to serve him as she could. Martha trusted in the person of Jesus—"I know God will give *you* whatever you ask." Hers was a simple faith that manifested itself in a service of simplicity.

Another Way

The little house in Bethany was Martha's world. To live and work and serve the Lord within its walls was all and enough for her. But she could not understand why it was not enough for her sister. She found it hard to see that there might be another way.

Mary shared Martha's faith in Jesus, but she was not content with a discipleship of sitting and knitting. This sister also had a deep hunger for the truth in Christ, but she needed more than small talk with him or the challenge of household chores for her expression of it. For Mary, the better part of serving was to listen and to learn and to seek out the revealed Word of God in Jesus. As Martha kept house for his humanity, Mary anointed his divinity. Each in her own way gave an offering of self, but they found it difficult to understand and accept each other.

Martha's way troubled Mary. "Why is she always so busy with things that don't matter? When will she learn to go beyond the pots and pans, the pillow under his head, and the constant cup of tea? How can I make her stop fussing to listen and learn the truth with me?"

Mary's way troubled Martha. "Why can't she accept him as he is and wait on him? He'll show his mystery to us in his own good time, in his own way. Why can't she simply trust him as I trust him—and help me with the dishes?"

The Lord Needs Us All

You recognize these sisters, don't you? Their separate devotion to Jesus the Christ is still seen in the church today among men and women. There are people in every congregation who are chiefly concerned about the church's housekeeping. Bills must be paid, the altar must look just right, buildings must be kept in good repair, things should be kept in order. They give themselves to this task with a selfless devotion, and their service of simple things is a necessary part of the church's life.

Then there are those who would look deeper into life and the meaning of things. They are concerned about explorations of faith and a study of its affirmations. With an equally selfless dedication, they give themselves to the task of learning the truth and witnessing to it at home with the family and out in the hostile world.

In some places, thanks be to God, Martha and Mary have rubbed off on each other and their ways are no longer separate or mutually exclusive. More and more these days you will find Martha leading a study group and Mary with a paintbrush in her hand.

But in too many parts of the church, Martha still fusses in her kitchen, Mary still insists on "in-depth discussion"; and sisters and brothers in the faith have not yet learned that Martha needs Mary, Mary needs Martha, and the Lord loves each one and needs them all in the whole work of his church.

The Canaanite Woman

"So Jesus said to her, 'For such an answer you may go home; the demon has gone out of your daughter!' "

Matthew 15:21-28
Mark 7:24-30

She had tried everything. She had gone everywhere, tracing every faint hope of healing for her little girl. And up and down the coast her anguish had been exploited. One hoax led to another, but she never stopped trying and hoping. Like most mothers, she was consumed with love for her little one. Her child's fever burned on her own brow. Her little girl's cries could be heard in her own sobbing. She felt her baby's torment in her own bones and blood. Driven by love she pursued her quest for healing, but inevitably she became more cautious and more cynical.

When she came to Jesus, she came hoping for the best but prepared for another disappointment. They told her, "There is one of whom it is said he gives sight to the blind, cleansing to the leper, and he can cast out demons!" It all sounded so painfully familiar. But one thing was different. "He does not ask for gold, not a penny will he seek. But," they said, "he is a Jew in the tradition of Moses and the prophets, and if you hope to have his help you must go with the words of Israel's faith upon your lips."

To tell the truth, at this point she cared little about Israel and its faith, but compelled by her love for her child, she was ready to say anything and to do whatever was necessary. To one who had spent her life's savings on charlatans and quacks, the mouthing of prescribed words and phrases seemed little enough to ask. In no time at all she made up her mind, learned the key words, and set out to find the no-charge healer from Galilee.

He was not easy to find. The truth is he was trying to stay out of sight for a while. In Jerusalem and in all Judea his name was on everyone's lips. The crowds followed him day and night, and the temple authorities who had been restless and uneasy about him from the first were now in an outrage at his attacks upon their ancient laws and their own blatant hypocrisy. In the Master's mind it was a time for lying low, for letting the storm clouds pass. So they found a nondescript house on an obscure street in a little-nothing town near the coastal city of Tyre. "He did not want anyone to know he was there . . .

". . . but he could not stay hidden." The healing grace of God in Christ cannot be kept from those who know of its power and who feel the compelling need of it in their own lives or in the lives of those they love.

The Canaanite woman followed up every rumor, listened for every new clue, and, as she came closer and closer, the disappointments on the way only served to strengthen her conviction that she was on the right track at last. Finally she went from village to village and then from house to house until she came to the place where Jesus was. But even then her struggle was not ended.

They would not let her in. They had their orders, after all. No doubt Peter was in charge, and Peter, with a little authority, must have been a tough man to beat. But she persisted, as a woman will. She wept and pleaded. She let her love for her child spill out before them all, and finally, defeated by her tears—"she keeps crying after us"—they let her in. And she fell at Jesus' feet and spoke the words she had been coached to speak: "Have mercy on me, Son of David." They had worked for others. They just might work for her.

But no. She was turned away. And we feel ourselves rebuffed. Why was Jesus so harsh with her? Why did he put her down so? He does not sound like the Lord we know. He would not even speak to her at first. That seems so unlike him. And when he did speak up, his words were hardly comforting or even courteous.

But the Canaanite woman did not feel the offense we feel. She knew from his silence that he knew what was in her heart. This Jewish holy man could see into her inmost soul. He knew she had not sought him in faith and in her heart he was not the "Son of David" as she had testified. He was not the Messiah promised, the very Christ her Lord. She knew that from the moment she started out. And now she knew that he knew. He was a means to an end, a last chance, a hope against hope. When Jesus told her that he could not give the "children's bread to dogs," she understood what he was saying. The healing grace of God is not offered willy-nilly to every taker. Faith in the Christ, the God of grace, must be present in those who seek his favor.

The Canaanite mother was not offended by the Master's hard words. She acknowledged the truth in them and confessed her own unworthiness. But, driven by her love, she made bold to ask if it were possible that some few crumbs of grace might fall to those who have not come to faith but who have learned the lesson of love. Are there times, O Christ, when love will answer where faith has not yet spoken, and is it possible that such selfless love is the open way to saving faith?

She had not come to Christ believing, that is true, but love, sweet love, had led her through thick and thin to the Savior's feet. "The dogs eat the crumbs that fall from their Master's table." She humbled herself before him and offered up, at that moment, not total faith but selfless love, and Jesus said, "For such an answer you may go home—you are a woman of great faith—what you want will be done for you."

The experience of the Canaanite woman with Jesus offers both a word of caution and a word of hope to us in our seeking him. In the first place, be careful not to make Jesus a means to some end. Too many of us look to him too often as an eraser of our own mistakes, a cure-all for self-inflicted wounds. No. We must come to faith in Jesus the Christ, the Savior of our souls, the Living Word of the promise of life eternal—and all these things will be added unto us.

But when faith fails—and you know how it does—take heart and remember that often selfless love can open the way to faith. And for Christ, as for his apostle Paul, faith, hope, and love abide, but the greatest of these is love.

The Woman at the Well

"Jesus answered . . . 'Whoever drinks the water that I will give him will never be thirsty again.'"

John 4:3-30

Jacob's well stood at a crossroads five miles or more outside the town of Sychar in Samaria. Though it still held good, clear water in its reservoir, by the time of Jesus it was more a shrine than a working well. According to tradition, Father Jacob in the ancient past had bought this tract of land, dug the well, and left it to Joseph, his favored son. Joseph, when he died, was carried back from Egypt and buried there. The old scriptures told about the well (Genesis 33:18-19, 48:52; Joshua 24:32); an atmosphere of holy history surrounded it.

But its sacred past meant nothing to the woman of Sychar. She preferred Jacob's well above the more convenient fountain in the marketplace only because it was remote. Especially at midday, she had it all to herself. And that's the way she wanted it, far from prying eyes and wagging tongues.

The Thirst

She had made a mess of her life, and she knew it. As far back as she could remember, there had always been a restlessness within her, a nameless, unsatisfied longing, a vague discontent, a thirst that would not be quenched. She went through life as one possessed, seeking her peace in all the wrong places. Thinking her thirst a thing of the senses, she sought relief in sensuality, eating and drinking and trying so hard to be merry. She went from spree to spree, from bed to bed; she made vows and quickly broke them. Her little fibs became outright lies, and all were woven finally into a fabric of infidelity. Loving and being loved gave way to a sordid using and being used. And with it all she became cynical and contemptuous of God and man. She lost her self-esteem. She lost herself.

The Discovery

When she came to Jacob's well that morning, it never occurred to her that Jesus would reach out in her direction. He was a man, a Jew, a respected rabbi. She was a woman, a Samaritan, living in sin. The walls of separation between them were high and wide ... and yet. ...

"Give me a drink of water," he said. And in the confrontation that followed, the woman at the well in Samaria found herself and God.

Her Sinful Self

In Jesus' presence she found herself and the reality of her own sin. He had a way of cutting through the conventional rationalization. He looked her in the eye, and she could not put the guilt off onto someone or something else as she usually did. Her parents and her early childhood, her first husband and his lack of understanding, her mother-in-law and her intrusions, the "changing morality," the "sexual liberation," the community's hypocrisy and prejudice—all these had played a part in shaping her lifestyle, but in the Lord's presence she saw at last that she was personally accountable for her own condition. With his eyes upon her and his spirit probing hers, she saw the truth about herself as she had never seen it before. In the presence of Jesus, the woman at the well found herself at last, a sinner in need of forgiveness, a sinner in need of God.

The Living Water

And when Jesus came, the woman of Sychar found in him peace for her troubled spirit, answers to her anxious questions, and the living water of God's forgiveness and grace for her sin-parched soul. He spoke the words to her: "Whoever drinks the water that I will give him will never be thirsty again. For the water that I will give him will become in him a spring [of] living water ... [of] eternal life." But more than the words, his very presence—the calm strength, the ring of authority in his voice, the gentle assurance of genuine love—all gave her to know that in Jesus the Christ, mysteriously, she was face to face with God.

The Real Presence

Few of the people around Jesus have as much to tell about him and his effect upon them as the woman at the well in Samaria. Space does not permit a full examination of all the many facets of this story. The most important word is this: When the Lord, in

Word and Sacrament, comes in his real presence, a sinner finds himself and his God. Face to face with Jesus, we are forced to see the reality of our own sinful natures and our personal accountability for the wrong we have done. At the same time, in the presence of Jesus we are given to know that God has not forsaken us in our sin; we are forgiven, redeemed, refreshed by the living water of his grace.

The Widow of Nain

"When the Lord saw her his heart was filled with pity for her and he said to her, 'Don't cry.' "

Luke 7:11-15
John 11:20-27

That young man's funeral in Nain was very different from the funerals you have attended. Traditions and customs, so commonplace then, seem rather strange to us today. Burial took place within twenty-four hours after death and before sundown. There was no "viewing." (Were they wiser than we?) The body was wrapped head to toe in a winding sheet and carried on a pallet or in an open wickerwork casket. There were no hired limousines or carriages; everyone walked. In place of the professional director of funerals there were paid mourners who moaned and wailed and wept salt tears on cue—if you did not hire them, people would say you really didn't care. In many ways that funeral in Nain was different from those we know.

But the feelings were the same. You would have recognized them. Like the catch in the throat and the loss for words. Only a year or so ago you walked beside this same grief-stricken friend when her husband died. How long was it? *You* forget, but *she* remembers. On that sad occasion you used up all the platitudes. "He is at peace." "Thank God for the years you had together." "It's a blessing—for his sake." "Accept God's will." You even remember saying to that young man at her side, "Now you are the head of the house, son; take care of your mother, you're all she has." What can you say now? Her old scars of grief have been cruelly torn open and she is alone. Your tongue clings to the roof of your mouth. You want to say, "Don't cry," but your own tears won't let you. You want to say, "Have hope," but your own hopelessness ties your tongue.

The Same Feeling

The funeral in Nain was different in the external things, but you recognize the feelings, don't you? The failure of words and then . . . the helplessness. What can you do? Bring a bowl of fruit, a garland of flowers. Prepare a meal for returning family and friends. And when at last you leave to go home to your living loved ones, feel the tearing at your heart as you say, "If there's anything else I can do. . . ."

Times change, our ways and our customs differ, but the deeper human feelings when death comes are now as they always were—the loss of words, the helplessness, and the bitter recognition of the inevitability of death in our own lives. We grieve with our stricken friends, but always a part of our grief is reserved unto ourselves. We know that this day and this long walk must come sooner or later to us all. The unanswerable questions, the empty chair, the finality of these farewells—we all must face them one day. At a funeral we are confronted by our own mortality, and we are reminded again that in the midst of life we are in death.

Twice Bereaved

The widow of Nain. That is all we know about her. She is not named. She is not described in any other way but that she was a grief-stricken mother, twice bereaved. As the story goes, she made her way along the now-too-familiar road, out of the city and up to the open vault. And Jesus came to her, a total stranger. Those who were there said later, "He felt so sorry for her. When he went to her, his face was contorted with grief. He opened his mouth as if to wail with the performing mourners, but the pained silence that came forth was more shrill than all their cries together. His heart went out to her and then, when he took her hand, in a sudden moment, there came a great peace over him. She felt it too. We all did. And when he spoke to her at last his voice came clear and strong with not the trace of a stammer. 'Mother, don't cry,' he said."

Well, of course that was just what nearly everyone else had said, but strange to tell, when *he* said it, it was different. His voice had the ring of authority. He seemed to know something about life and death that she did not know. He was in possession of some power over grief which she and all the rest had not yet discovered.

The Compassion of God

"Don't cry," Jesus said. He brought to the weeping widow the compassion of God. Only Jesus the Christ could do that. He revealed to her in that stirring moment on her road of sorrows the mysterious truth that God walked it with her and with all grieving souls. God shares our emptiness, our loneliness; he suffers through the torments of death with us. The widow of Nain, it must be understood, was consoled and strengthened and given new hope *before* the miracle happened. Surely she could not comprehend in all parts what was taking place, but the presence of the Son of God beside her in the graveyard, his hand on hers, his Word coming clear, made all the difference and turned her sorrow into singing, her mourning into dancing.

The Resurrection and the Life

"Don't cry," Jesus said. And when *he* said it, she knew that she was hearing more than words. She knew, she felt, Jesus *is* the Word. He is the resurrection and the life, and when you believe in him, you will live even though you die, and whoever lives and believes in him will never die.

V

The
Outsiders

Friends and Foes Beyond the Fringe

A man is known by the friends he makes ... and keeps. But a man is also known by his enemies and by the enemies he converts to friendship.

Jesus made many friends. His ministry of preaching and healing drew people of all kinds to his side. But he made enemies too. His forthright attacks upon hypocrisy in high places, his determination to reveal the immorality and blasphemy behind the mask of Pharisaic self-righteousness and religious display, and his uncompromising demand for love and justice in all relationships caused first a murmuring, then a contrived whispering campaign to discredit his ministry, and eventually a conscious effort to destroy him.

In viewing the people around Jesus, a study of the outsiders, friends and foes and foes become friends, is essential. They help us to see the strong, uncompromising side of the Master's character. They show us the unfailing persistence of his compassionate, forgiving love.

Nicodemus, intellectual skeptic and high-born Pharisee, was suspicious of the Nazarene carpenter-turned-rabbi. But Jesus put new thoughts in his mind and new dreams in his heart, and though he continued to follow beyond the fringe, at the last he came to the cross in faith.

Zacchaeus, guilt-ridden, stunted in spirit, thought himself unworthy, beyond saving. He dared not come close to this Jesus of the healing hands and the gentle heart and the Word of God in his mouth. But the Lord found him up a tree and brought him back to earth and offered him a life worth living.

Malchus, the high priest's servant, knew nothing and cared less about Jesus. With the soldiers and the rabble he "came out with swords and clubs" to capture an outlaw. He returned shaken to the depths of his soul by the Lord's demonstration of love, even for his enemies.

Simon of Cyrene wanted no part in that first passion play. But under the cross, sharing the shame and the pain and the burden, walking in the bloodstained footprints of Jesus, he was a new man, born again!

Some of these outsiders whose experiences are recounted in the following pages were outright enemies of Jesus at the start. Others, though not openly opposed, were nevertheless beyond the fringe of friendship and support. Their response to him and the change which came over them when they came under his influence can draw us closer to the Christ and provide new insights for our present-day understanding of his grace and power.

Zacchaeus, Low Man on Top

"There was a chief tax collector there, named Zacchaeus, who was rich."
Luke 19:1-10
Luke 18:24-25

The people in that crowd in Jericho when Jesus came "passing through" were much like the crowd people in every city and town along his way. They were "just folks," ordinary people of modest means: day laborers, civil servants, marketplace merchants, housekeepers and mothers. In simple, nondescript houses they lived their simple, nondescript lives. They were "average-income" people, except for the beggars and vagrants and other community parasites. These were a crowd within the crowd, always coming in great numbers, especially since word had gotten out about Jesus' way with a few loaves of bread and a couple of fish.

It was a typical crowd of typical common people, and they were, for the most part, quiet, orderly, and congenially accepting of one another. They showed great tolerance, possibly because everyone had someone to look down upon. No matter how bad things were, you could always find someone in the crowd who was worse off—more crippled, more lonely, more guilty, more destitute. Tolerance in a community is often nothing more than collective condescension. They were able to rub shoulders with one another because they were all on the same level or a step above their nearest neighbor.

Enter Zacchaeus

That is probably why, when Zacchaeus tried to join in, they shouldered him out and cut him off. They had permitted a dwarf beggar with his card tricks to waddle through to the front line. They even lifted him high for a better view. But when Zacchaeus came, they stood tall and closed ranks and kept him beyond the rim.

Sin or Success?

They would not tolerate *him*, they said, because he was a crooked politician, a graft-taker, a swindler, and a thief. The truth is that most of them were guilty, at one time or another, of the same sins, but they operated at a much lower level and at much less profit. They resented Zacchaeus because he had won at the game which most of them played. Had he been crooked but poor, they would have welcomed him as one of their own.

But Zacchaeus was rich. He had everything money could buy: a grand house in town and a country place, with indoor plumbing in both! The best cuts of meat, the rarest of wines, servants at his side at the snap of a finger, custom-tailored clothes, rings on his fingers—Zacchaeus was rich. What was he doing here? Why didn't he stay up on the hill where he belonged?

Low Man on Top

Luke tells this story with such exquisite irony. Zacchaeus, short in stature, is looked down upon and physically shut out of the community because they resent, all of them, not his sin but his success, and they sense that he has risen above them and attained a height which is beyond their grasp. They feel the little man looking down on them, and their tolerance vanishes.

The story of Zacchaeus puts a new light on the words of Jesus: "How hard it is for a rich man to enter the kingdom of God." Perhaps the Lord is saying here that it is difficult for men of means to become significant parts of the church's life because common people of modest means too often close ranks against them, directly or indirectly doing all they can to keep them out.

Up and Out

Zacchaeus is a perfect example of a man who is "up and out," cut off from the presence of Jesus and separated from the community of faith by the suspicion and the resentment and the envy which his wealth and position arouse in the hearts and minds of those who are in the community. When that little rich man Zacchaeus came looking for Jesus that day, it is just possible that he was more highly motivated in his quest than all the rest of that crowd put together. He came out of curiosity, as they all did, but he was not looking for a magic bread maker or a healer of crippled limbs or a miraculous catch of fish.

Zacchaeus ran on ahead and climbed a tree for a better view of Jesus, because it was said of him, "He can change your life, he can make you over, he will forgive you and you will know in your heart of hearts that you are forgiven of God; he will fill you with a joy that all the gold and glory cannot give; he will save your soul." Zacchaeus went out on a limb to see the Lord in spite of all the crowd's attempts to keep him away, and Jesus came, called him down, blessed his house, and made him feel like he was ten feet tall!

Come Down!

Christians are called to witness and to welcome into their fellowship *all* men, the poor and the needy, the rich and the needy, for Christ came to seek and to save the lost on every level of human existence. Yet in our work and witness we have frequently ignored or actually denied our responsibility to those on the better side of town. ("They really don't want to bother with us anyway!") We are often suspicious, envious, fearful, insecure in their presence, so we close ranks with the people we know and understand, and the seeking soul in the house on the hill is subtly excluded from our community of faith.

Perhaps there is a need in your church and in your community to evangelize the up and out and to speak these words of the Lord again: "Zacchaeus, come down! Salvation has come to *your* house today!"

Nicodemus, Hidden Disciple

" 'How can this be?' asked Nicodemus."

John 3:1-10
John 7:50
John 19:39

A gentle wind was blowing as he made his way down the dark street and up the narrow outside staircase of the small town house. In the nighttime stillness the scuffle of his sandals on the stairs made his presence known, and the door of the rooftop room opened silently even as he reached to knock upon it. Entering, he stood face to face at last with the strange Galilean whose coming had uncovered hidden questions in his heart.

Nicodemus—wealthy son of a wealthy father; he had not been spoiled by his easy inheritance. His whole life had been spent in the study of the Law and in the preservation of it. One of the elite corps of intellectual Pharisees, he was a ranking member of the ruling Sanhedrin. The Law of Moses and the traditions of the Fathers comprised the sacred code by which he lived. The way to God for Nicodemus was the path of absolute obedience. The will of God was done when the Law was fulfilled in each minute detail. The kingdom of God would come by "Thou shalt!" and "Thou shalt not!" Nicodemus genuinely believed what the old rabbis had set down: "The law is complete; it contains everything necessary for the living of the good life. Therefore there must be a rule and regulation to govern every possible incident in every possible moment of life for every possible man."

Jesus' Higher Law

But then Jesus came, calling God "Father" and proclaiming a new and higher law—the law of love. His words, as they filtered back to Nicodemus, were a strange mixture. They caught the Pharisee coming and going. On the one hand, Jesus said that "the least point or the smallest detail of the Law will not be done away with (Matt. 5:18)," and Nicodemus approved. On the other hand, the Master said, "Pharisees! You are like whitewashed tombs . . . on the outside you appear to everybody as good, but inside you are full of lies and sins (Matt. 23:27-28)." Such talk had enraged Nicodemus' colleagues. The exclusive Pharisaic fraternity was convinced that it must close in on this Jesus and silence him for good.

But Nicodemus felt an uneasy awareness of truth in Jesus' words, and he chose to play a waiting game. He listened and he watched and as the days passed, almost against his own will, he found himself drawn to the Nazarene. Finally he decided to see him face to face and have it out with him once and for all.

Curious but Not Committed

But he dare not let it be known. If it should come out that he had sought Jesus and talked with him, he himself would be ostracized. The world he knew would cut him cold. His circle of friends, well manicured, intelligent, sophisticated, affluent, "the beautiful people," would turn their backs on him. He felt an overpowering curiosity about Jesus, but he was not about to change his whole life-style for the sake of some preaching carpenter from Nazareth.

The thought of total heart-mind-soul commitment to the Way of Jesus never entered his mind. So he came under cover of darkness, alone and incognito.

Confronted by the Christ

Standing there in the lantern light, Nicodemus felt, from the first, at a disadvantage. He had come, an inquirer. Or, to put it more truthfully, an inquisitor. Now, under the Master's steady gaze, he felt *himself* under scrutiny, suspect and vulnerable. He had come to discuss theological principles and religious propositions, points of law and philosophies of life. He wanted a conflict of ideas, a wrestling match of minds, an intellectual exercise. Instead, as he stood before the man Jesus, he found himself in a spiritual confrontation with the Christ of God.

God's Way

Whether we like it or not, that is always the way of God in Christ. He *will* bring us face to face with the mystery of his free grace. He *will* force us to ask not "how" but "who," and he will insist on a personal confrontation with his Spirit. Ultimately he comes to us in our naked selfhood, calling us to faith in the mystery of his saving love and in the transforming power of his

Holy Spirit. "No one can see the Kingdom of God unless he is born again . . . of water and the Spirit." When Jesus put that proposition before Nicodemus, so abruptly at the very start of their conversation, he cut through all the Pharisee's prepared arguments for righteousness by the law, the coming of the kingdom by legislation.

A man is made over—reborn, transformed, converted—not by his own deeds, however good they seem; not by his own gifts, however generous; not by his own meticulous adherence to moral codes and ethical standards, however strict; not by his own exalted testimony of religious fantasies, however otherworldly they may be; a man is born again by the reconciling love of God. Redemption is *the* act of God. It is not the result of man's accumulated acts, "being good" and "doing what is right." The new life of the Christian is all God's doing. His Spirit, like the night wind in Jerusalem, "blows wherever it wishes but you do not know where it comes from or where it is going." But when you have been touched by the Spirit, you surely know that a mighty act of God has happened—you are born again, a new being, and life can never be the same.

The Question

"How can this be?" asked Nicodemus. And so do we. Like him, we often try to intellectualize our faith. We want things all spelled out in foolproof formulas. And, like Nicodemus, we would rather work it out ourselves than take the risk of faith, trusting only in God's love.

So the struggle goes on and the question is asked again and again—how? Until at last with Nicodemus we are brought to Calvary, where the heart accepts what the mind could never comprehend, and there in the death of Christ we are made alive.

Malchus, the Wounded Enemy

"He touched the man's ear and healed him."

John 18:1-11
Luke 22:47-51
Matthew 5:38-48

He has little more than a walk-on part in the drama of the Lord's last days. The man named Malchus appears on stage for one brief moment, takes a glancing blow, and is gone. His role as one of the people around Jesus seems so small, so insignificant. What can we hope to learn from this bit player in the passion of our Lord?

The scriptural record itself is brief and direct. Malchus was a servant of the high priest. On that night of the Lord's betrayal he came to Gethsemane with the squad of temple guards under the high priest's orders. There is a real possibility that Malchus was there simply out of curiosity or in search of some excitement. No doubt in the gossip halls of the high priest's household he had heard many wild tales about this faith healer of Galilee. Now he had the chance to see for himself and to be part of the action besides.

That is really all we know about this man. But it is enough because Malchus is important to us, not for what we may learn about *him* but for the insight which his experience offers regarding Jesus and the Way.

Remembering

Often as the years went by, Malchus must have recalled that night in the garden. Whenever in rain or cold he felt the faint throbbing in that scar on his ear, the whole scene must have flashed again upon the wide screen of his memory. Then he would think, with a wry smile, of Simon Peter's clumsy swordsmanship and, in greater depth, of the living word of love with which Jesus had touched him.

Malchus remembered how when they came to Gethsemane he had worked his way to the front of the temple contingent, watching for Iscariot and his kiss signal. Then, just when he had expected a chase through the garden, the Nazarene, in complete command of himself and of the situation, had come forward, saying, "Who is it you are looking for? Here I am!"

After that it was all confusion. Malchus remembered watching Simon struggling to get his borrowed sword out of its sheath. The hilt caught in his waistband, and it was plain to see that he was new at the game. At any rate, he didn't scare anybody. There was a lot of noise and distraction, a scuffling and a shouting among the Nazarene's men, and then suddenly, out of the torchlight smoke, Simon came like a charging bull lunging toward them.

They all scattered, laughing and catcalling as they ducked and hit the ground. But Simon's temper was up and his sword lashed out, thrusting and thrashing in a crazy, haphazard way. Malchus remembered trying to get out of range and suddenly the quick sharp pain and the wet warmth of his own blood on his neck.

Malchus remembered how Jesus had come to him then, with comfort and healing in his hands. The blood stopped flowing, the pain over his whole right side began to recede, and Malchus knew that his life would never be the same again.

The Incredible Commandment

In later years, running his finger down the lines of the old scar, Malchus remembered how Jesus had given meaning and truth to his own incredible commandment, "Love your enemy. Do good to those who hate you. Bless those who curse you. Pray for those who mistreat you. Love your enemies and do good to them."

Malchus had felt in his own body the possibility of Jesus' impossible idea. The very words, "Love your enemy," had come alive for him in the healing of his own wounds. There in the garden on the Mount of Olives, the high priest's servant caught a glimpse of love through the eyes of God. "Greater love has no man than *this*, that he give up his life—for his *enemy*."

More than Passive Resistance

It was given to Malchus to see, as few men ever do, that the love and peace of which Jesus speaks call for more than a refusal to fight back. Christ's way is more than a passive resistance. It is a visible reaching out and a tangible caring for those who stand against us. It offers not only the end of hostility but, far beyond that, the healing of the wounded enemy. And if men could only see this and make a real try at it, they could, as Jesus promised, change the world.

Undoubtedly, Malchus after his healing in Gethsemane saw everyone, friend and foe, through different eyes. You cannot go on in the old way when you have been forgiven as he was forgiven, befriended as he was, healed by the very hands you have come to bind. When you have felt such an impossible love on your own wounds, your eyes are opened to the wounds that you must heal, to the forgiveness that you must offer, to the impossible love that is possible for you.

The Symbol of Ourselves

We know so little of Malchus, but we may learn so much from his experience with Jesus. He is, as in a parable, the symbol of ourselves. In our raw nature we all stand before God in enmity, opposing his will, profaning his name, defiling his earth, rejecting his love. Wonder of wonders, he does not turn away from us.

No. Incredibly he continues to ask, "Who is it you are looking for?" And when we fall away in shame, he comes and comes again, reaching out and down with his impossible love, touching our enmity with the healing friendship of his grace. We'll never be the same again!

Simon of Cyrene, the Crossbearer

"They seized him, put the cross on him and made him carry it behind Jesus."
Mark 15:21
Luke 23:26
Luke 9:23-24

Life looks different from under a cross. Beneath the weight of it and the pain of it and the shame of it, your whole perspective changes. Under a cross, you get a new view of yourself, of those around you, and even of God.

Oh, at first it's all self-pity and resentment. You find yourself asking, "Why? Why *me*? With so many others standing around, why should I be the one to take it? What have I done? Where did I go wrong? Why pick on me?"

In those early moments of crossbearing, the injustice of the whole affair very nearly overwhelms you. Anyone you can think of seems more deserving of such a fate than you. They've all been more faithless, more sinful, more loveless, more hateful—yet they go scot free and even seem to prosper. It's all so unfair, so unjust. And no one seems to care. Not even God.

Yes. When you're new at crossbearing you usually spend some time blaming God. Trudging along, weary with the burden you've been forced to bear, every breath becomes a labored "if." If God is good, if God is love, if God is God—this would not be. This could not be. And you end up tormented with the fear that God is gone or that he never was.

Discovery Beneath a Cross

Yet there's something about carrying a cross. The very weight of it makes you go through life more slowly. And the slower pace forces you to look more carefully at yourself, at those around you, and even at God.

When you look at life from beneath a cross you discover things about yourself that you simply did not know or ever would have known. You get a new view of what is essential to your life and what is not: titles and tax shelters, dividends and interest rates, the newest travel machine, a place in the country, and lots of insurance. And, oh, to be "in" and to go abroad and to be privately country-clubbed! So many things that mattered so much, matter so little beneath a cross.

Then, too, crossbearing brings out the real strength that is in you. Most of us go through life using only part of our powers. So much intellect and spirit and sheer physical strength is dissipated by neglect. Often only the weight of a heavy cross will force us to extend ourselves, to stretch and know our own strength.

Companions in Suffering

Beneath a cross the view is different. You learn new and deep truths about yourself and about others, too. You cannot go far on the road of sorrows before it comes to you that you are not alone. You begin to see, as you did not see before, how many other crossbearers there are along the way. To be sure, some of them are unaware of the burden that is upon them; weighed down and troubled, they know not why. Beneath the cross, through your own tears, you can see and recognize the suffering in other eyes. It takes a crossbearer to know a crossbearer. Only those who have walked this burdened way have the vision and the strength to reach out to their companions in suffering.

The Ultimate Discovery

Life looks different from under a cross. You see yourself and others with fresh eyes. And eventually you learn the truth about God. He has not left you or forsaken you as you feared. No. See—he is the bleeding stranger who leads the way to Calvary. That's God up there with the thorny crown and the sorrowing love in his eyes. You are walking in God's footprints! And he knows. He knows what it is to bear a cross, the weight of it and the pain of it and the shame of it.

Beneath a cross—perhaps *only* beneath a cross—may we learn the blessed truth that God goes before us on the road of sorrows. Crossbearing leads at last to this ultimate discovery of God: "Christ himself carried our sins on his body to the cross, so that we might die to sin and live for righteousness (1 Peter 2:24)." *We* carry a cross, but *he* suffers and dies upon it—for us!

From Cyrene to Calvary

Simon the crossbearer is another one of the little-known people around Jesus. We know his name. We know where he hailed from: Cyrene in North Africa on the shore of the Mediterranean, in those times a ten-day journey to Jerusalem. Another significant point recorded in the Gospel of Mark is that this Simon was the "father of Alexander and Rufus," two young men whose names appear among the leaders of the early Christian church in other New Testament writings.

Simone of Cyrene, an ordinary man on the street who first came to Jesus against his will, beneath a cross he had not sought and did not want. We feel a special kinship with him. His experience on the road of sorrows can lift us up along our troubled way. In crossbearing he found himself, and so can we. Beneath the cross he encountered others in pain and in need, and so must we. On the way to Calvary Simon of Cyrene discovered God in Christ his Savior, and so shall we!

"If anyone wants to come with me, he must forget himself, take up his cross every day, and follow me!"

VI

Disciples-Come-Lately

Faith Makes the Difference

Not all the people around Jesus were eyewitnesses. Not all his disciples were privileged to walk and talk with him in Galilee and Judea. The Holy Spirit of God, moving in the hearts of men and women down through the years, has brought new followers generation after generation. These latter-day disciples are "people around Jesus" just as surely as were they who saw him face to face.

Some of them, extraordinary Christians, are known to us by name and reputation. The record of their work and witness for the Christ has been preserved for us. Augustine, Athanasius, Chrysostom, Boniface, Francis of Assisi, Thomas a Kempis, John Huss, Savonarola, Martin Luther, John Calvin, Charles Wesley, Dietrich Bonhoeffer—from the first century to the twentieth, the lives of these sainted Christians show us how the Christ still draws human hearts unto himself and changes the direction of many lives.

A complete study of all these disciples-come-lately must wait for another day. In these pages, it must suffice to look at but two of them: the best known and earliest, Paul of Tarsus, the missionary apostle; and, at the other end of the time line, perhaps the least known . . . the disciple in your mirror. Paul and you—representations of the post-Pentecost people around Jesus.

Paul, the Apostle

"Is not this the man who made havoc in Jerusalem . . . ?"*
Acts 9:1-30
2 Corinthians 11:21—12:10

When he first came to Jesus his name was Saul, and he came not as a friend but as a sworn enemy. If anyone had told him in those early days that soon he would proclaim Jesus the Christ across the wide world's boundaries and give his life in this cause, Saul would have called it the devil's own prophecy. But suddenly, along the way, the light of the Almighty blinded his eyes, the hand of God held him fast, and in a moment of conversion glory the foe became a friend—Saul became Paul.

Among all the people around Jesus, before and after Pentecost, never a man or a woman changed so radically as did the apostle to the Gentiles. But did he—really? Was the Paul who came, sightless and Spirit-led, to Damascus entirely different from the Saul who had started out from Jerusalem "breathing threats and murder against the disciples of the Lord (Acts 9:1, RSV)"?

He didn't look any different. He was no taller, no shorter. His voice hadn't changed, or the color of his eyes. He had the same fingerprints. Paul was Saul. In most ways, he was the very same man. All the characteristics, all the gifts, all the strengths and weaknesses were still very much the same. Saul's training in systematic thought and the processes of Jewish law were an important part of Paul's apostolic equipment. Saul's cosmopolitan origin and rearing—the religion of the Jews, the culture of the Greeks, the politics of Rome—were important factors in Paul's ministry. Saul's impatience with inaction was a heat that coursed through Paul's veins, too. Saul's self-conceit and pride were often reflected in Paul's self-glorifying, no matter how hard he tried to cover it up with a mask of humility.

Even the fanaticism was the same. There was nothing that would hinder Paul from doing the Christian work he had to do. The wild mountains of Greece, the unknown depths of the inland sea, the throbbing in his head and the fever in his own flesh, even

---
* Acts 9:21, RSV.

the cold chains and the headsman's ax—none could put down or quiet the clamoring in his breast. Paul the apostle was a man on fire.

But look! So was Saul when he persecuted Christ's apostles. Saul had the same get-up-and-go, the same fervor. He never rested either from the task he was committed to do. Night and day he hunted them down, those first-century Jesus freaks. Up and down the streets of Jerusalem and out into its suburbs he went like a man possessed. Saul was on fire too.

Paul was Saul. Jesus saw in this enemy of the cross a potential apostle extraordinary, and by the Spirit's voice he called him forth. In turning him around and changing his name—take note of this—the Lord did not perform any plastic surgery or personality-changing miracle. He took him where he was. He took him as he was, *changing only his motivations and the direction of his life's powers.*

There is an important lesson about Christian commitment and discipleship in the story of Saul become Paul, the post-Pentecost apostle of Jesus. When the Master confronted him on the Damascus Road, he sought only to change the focus of his faith. In every conversion experience, faith is the critical factor. Jesus does not expect—indeed, he does not *want*—you to change your life-style except in those areas that are inconsistent with the Christian faith in your heart . . . and only you before God can be the judge of that . . . and only you with Christ can say what changes should be made. The Lord does not seek a loss of identity or a denial of selfhood in those who are called to discipleship. He does not want his faithful people to become carbon copies of one another, with the same sanctimonious look in every eye and a Bible in every hand.

Each of us brings different powers, various strengths, to the ministry of our Lord. We move in different spheres of influence. We touch different lives, we bring an infinite variety of natural gifts and developed skills, and each of us must learn to see himself as a potential apostle, ministering in a uniquely personal way.

When the conversion moment comes, Jesus says to us as he said to Paul, "If you believe in God and if you love me, then be yourself and do your own thing to the glory of God and the good of your brothers."

The Disciple in Your Mirror

The people around Jesus in the New Testament came to him at different moments in their lives. They came by separate ways and for many varied reasons. Some were led by others who had found him first; some came with desperate needs, looking for a miracle; many were simply curious and stood around on the edge of discipleship for a long time before they took the last sure leap of faith. Others, disillusioned with false gods and deceptive philosophies, sought him out finally as their last best hope.

How was it for you? Yes, you! Aren't you one of the people around Jesus today? How did it happen? What was it—who was it—that brought you to his side?

As a child you were taken one day to a learning room in a strange building. There were Jesus-pictures on the wall, and there, in stories from a book they called "The Bible," you heard about his love and learned to sing of it. Remember? You came to Jesus as a child, and you've been with him ever since.

But on the other hand, maybe it was not like that at all. Oh, you may have the same dear memories of old church rooms and holy pictures and "Jesus loves me, this I know," but even now, looking back, that was all part of a childhood fantasy. It never did become part of life as you knew it. When did *you* come to the Master's side? How was it for you? Can you remember?

A dark day. Walls of grief and loneliness falling in. "Hope" is a bitter word upon your tongue. A shroud of doubt and fear covers you. And in that moment of utter despair, a word begins to burn in the darkness, ever so dimly at first, then brighter and brighter. The word is "love," and it is Jesus the Lord who gives it burning life for you. You hear him say, "I am with you—always." And you believe. And here you are.

The people around Jesus come to him by different roads. Sometimes a little child leads us. "Daddy, come and see!" You go just to please the little fellow . . . one good word leads to another . . . until at last you feel at home there with Jesus' people. Sometimes you fall in love, and the object of your affection happens to be one of the people around Jesus, and in the company of love you discover Love at its highest and best in Jesus the Christ.

You are one of the people around Jesus. How did you get that way? Perhaps you cannot recall a certain time or place. For many of us, our relationship with the Lord is a gradually growing thing. We cannot recall a moment of light on a Damascus Road. Discipleship comes day by day in a slow and steady process of change; half a lifetime passes, and you wake one day and know that you belong to him. You are one of Jesus' people.

Well, are you? Have you surely found the Lord? Are you part of the company he keeps? How can you know for certain? How can you be sure?

In a very real way the reality of the Christian faith in our hearts and the Christian way in our lives is tested and proven best by their impact upon those who go through life with us. If you are in fact one of the people around Jesus, those who share the passing days with you should be the first to know it. When we truly come to the Lord, his effect upon us is felt first by those nearest. The new love touches first the hearts that are but a beat away. The new joy, peace, glory is shown first of all to them. When you do indeed become one of the people around Jesus, you begin to see things differently: needs you did not lift your hands to, wounds you made no move to heal, lonely hearts you had no time for.

The closer you get to Jesus, the closer you will want to get to those around you. When you really become one of Jesus' people, your father and your mother, your sister and your brother, your husband or your wife and children will know without being told that something has happened to you. The love of Jesus and all that goes with it—forgiveness, good humor, kindness, gentle courtesy, cheerful understanding—will touch them first. Anyone who thinks of himself as one of the people around Jesus can measure and test his discipleship by the honest opinion of his loved ones. If they have not noticed the presence of the Christ in you, the chances are that no one has, or will.

Are you one of the people around Jesus? There is really no purpose to the study of Jesus' people in the Gospels unless it leads us to see something of his presence and his power in our own lives.

To see the passing parade of men and women, children, and young people—the rich and the poor, the wise and the simple who walked and talked with the Lord in his days on earth—is of little significance in the long run unless their experience with Jesus sheds light upon our relationship with him.

To you as to Andrew and the other apostles, Jesus comes calling, "Follow me." To you as to Zacchaeus, Malchus, and Simon of Cyrene, Jesus comes, challenging, "Mend your ways and come my way." To you as to the women and the children of Galilee, Jesus comes with his blessed invitation, "Come unto me."

Take a long close look at yourself in the mirror of your loved ones' eyes. Seach your soul in the light of God's Word. Are you one of them—*the people around Jesus?*

Helps for
Further Study

A Shared Bible Study Guide for PEOPLE AROUND JESUS

Introduction

People Around Jesus can serve as the theme for a six-session study of Jesus' life and ministry, giving special attention to the impact of his personality and character upon the people around him. The New Testament and particularly the four Gospels provide the scriptural basis for the study. This guide suggests learning experiences for each of the six categories of people around Jesus. The "people stories" and other commentaries and dictionaries provide background information.

A Shared Study—What It Is

A shared Bible study is guided by a convener. This person serves as the organizer and general overseer of the study. He secures the necessary resource materials, arranges and publicizes the study schedule, enlists hosts and hostesses when sessions are held in private homes, appoints prayer leaders, and serves as the discussion starter and guide during the study sessions.

The convener is not a Bible teacher. He is not expected to have all the answers. He shares in the study along with every other participant. His role is primarily that of practical organizer and guide.

A shared study of the Bible is meant to be used in small groups of six to ten participants. When groups are larger than this, they should be divided into smaller subgroups. The small group enables every member to share in the prayers, the research, and the discussion of the texts. It encourages the more reticent to express their points of view, and it lends itself more readily to the friendly, informal atmosphere in which a true sharing experience may take place.

How to Go About It

1. *Before the Session.* The convener will notify all prospective participants of the time and place of the meeting. This is essential for the first two or three meetings. Thereafter the time and place of future meetings can be announced at the close of each

session. The convener will make certain that at least two of the suggested commentaries, a Bible dictionary and a selection of modern translations of the New Testament, are available for use at the meeting place. Each participant is expected to have his own copy of *People Around Jesus* and his Bible in the translation which he prefers.

2. *Study Elements.* The following is a general description of the study elements to be used in most of the sessions. When the group has been sharing together for two or three sessions, changes and adaptations can be made as the group sees fit.

Prayer. It is essential that those who search the scriptures together should call upon God's Holy Spirit for direction and guidance as they seek the truth in his word. However, prayer that is meaningful cannot be "scheduled." It must arise out of the mood and spirit of the group; it must be an expression of their feelings, their aspirations, their needs. At the first session, the convener should be prepared to serve as prayer leader. Thereafter, different members of the group should be encouraged to serve.

Getting started. Because the study deals especially with personal relationships and personal involvements with the people around us, it will be essential to develop a group identity—a feeling of belonging, an in-depth acquaintance of each member of the group with all the others. To this end, various exercises in getting acquainted have been suggested for the start of each meeting.

Discovering the people around us. This study of the different people around Jesus—how he met them, how he acted toward them, their response to him—will have greater meaning for us if we can see it in the context of our own lives and our own personal relationships.

Each of the six parts of this study includes learning processes in which participants examine and evaluate their own relationships with others—loved ones, co-workers, friends, casual acquaintances—in the light of similar relationships in the life of Jesus. In learning how Jesus acted and reacted in certain interpersonal relationships, participants should begin to see the things that are needful for a greater Christ-likeness in their own life and experience.

Searching the scriptures. One of the special goals of the textual study of the people around Jesus is to help participants see the importance of studying isolated verses of scripture in the light of the whole passage, chapter, and book in which they are found. Many of the people around Jesus in the Gospels are anonymous; they appear only briefly in passing references. Our insights about them and their relationships with the Christ must derive from the context of time and place and the variety of circumstances in which they appear.

Three textual study methods are suggested in this guide. After each has been tried, the group may wish to settle upon the one which best serves its own needs. In this textual study, regardless of the method used, *participants should do the research, record the findings, and share in drawing conclusions.* Concordances, Bible dictionaries, commentaries, and other resources should be available for reference when needed.

Talking it over. It will be important in the planning of each meeting to allow enough time for this final sharing of reactions to the learnings provided by the interpersonal processes and the textual study. Use the suggested stimulus questions provided for this part of each meeting. They will help participants in evaluating what they have learned about themselves as the people around Jesus today.

Suggested Resources

One-volume Commentaries:
The Abingdon Bible Commentary, ed. David G. Downey and others. Nashville, Tenn.: Abingdon Press, 1929.
Interpreter's One-Volume Commentary on the Bible. New York: Abingdon Press, 1967.
Peake's Commentary on the Bible, ed. Matthew Black and H. W. Rawley. New York: Thomas Nelson & Sons, 1962.

Individual Book Commentaries:
Daily Study Bible, ed. William Barclay. Philadelphia: Westminster Press (two volumes on Matthew and John, one each on Mark and Luke).
Layman's Bible Commentary. Richmond: John Knox Press, 1959-64.
The Interpreter's Bible. Nashville, Tenn.: Abingdon Press, 1951-57. Twelve vols. on Old and New Testaments.

Bible Dictionaries:
Harper's Bible Dictionary, ed. Madeleine S. Miller and J. Lane. New York: Harper & Brothers, 1952.
The Interpreter's Dictionary of the Bible. 4 vols. New York: Abingdon Press, 1962.
Hastings Dictionary of the Bible, ed. F. C. Grant and H. H. Rowley. Rev. ed. New York: Charles Scribner's Sons, 1963.

The Study

Part I.: Outer-circle Disciples

Getting Started. In this first session, the get-acquainted exercise will be part of the "Discovering" process (see below). Perhaps a word or two about the shared-study method, the role of the convener, and the schedule and location of future meetings should be offered at this point.

Discovering the People Around Us. If members of the group have known each other for any period of time or have met together in other group situations, let each person take a blank piece of paper and write his or her name at the top. Ask each person to write one word under his name which will help to set him apart—some unique characteristic which would help to identify him in the group. (It is important for the convener to participate fully in this activity.) Press for just one word (a hyphenated word may be allowed, but don't let anyone stretch it to a phrase or short sentence).

As soon as possible, begin passing the papers to the right, asking each person to add one significant fact which he knows about the person whose name is on the top of the page.

Two basic rules should be followed: (1) Avoid vague generalities like "She is a lovely lady." If some specific fact is not known about the person, leave it blank and pass the paper on to the next person. (A page which comes back around the circle half blank will give you an idea of where you need to work in getting to know each other.) (2) Do not repeat information already given on the page. Read what everyone else has written before adding your word. You may learn many interesting new things about your friends in the circle.

When all the papers have circled back to the person whose name is on the top of the page, have each one read what the group has written and then spend a few minutes talking it over. Are you surprised at the kinds of things identified by the group? Are there other bits of information you would like to share with the group to help them see a more balanced picture of you? Is there information that is not quite accurate which you would like to correct? As a total group, what kinds of things have members emphasized about each other, superficial things which make us all seem pretty much alike or in-depth things which illuminate persons as unique and important individuals?

After a brief discussion, tape the information sheets to the walls of your meeting place and encourage the group to add additional bits of information which they discover throughout this and the following sessions.

If some members of the group are strangers, divide the group into pairs, separating any two persons who already seem to know each other fairly well. Ask the persons in each pair to tell each other their names and briefly to describe what they would be doing at this particular time if they had not come to this study. Give the pairs about five minutes to talk. Then bring the group back together and let each person introduce his/her partner: "This is ____(name)____ , and he/she has made a real sacrifice to be here. . . ." Some of the introductions may be serious, some silly; the purpose is to get to know someone quickly and to validate the fact that in our busy lives the decision to give up something else to meet together says something about our interest in and commitment to the study we are about to undertake.

NOTE: It is again urgent that the convener not only give instructions for the introductions but participate actively in one of the pairs. If the group is uneven, put three persons in one group and let each introduce one of the others.

The time spent on either of these Discovery exercises will depend upon the length of time planned for each session. If the session is to be but an hour in length, this part will have to be comparatively brief, but if a two-hour session is planned, more time can be given here.

Searching the Scriptures—Resources-study Method. Assign a member of the group to use a concordance to find all the scriptural references to the person or persons under study. (The convener may decide in advance, or he may wish to let the group determine which and how many of the "Followers at a Distance" to investigate.) As the concordance searcher announces the texts, another member of the group should list the references on a chalk board or piece of newsprint while the rest of the group finds and reads the passages.

Have the group take note of any place names or the names of other persons in the texts. These should also be listed on the board and checked for further references in the concordance.

Assign other members of the group to find and record information about the texts, about the person under study, and about the place names mentioned. Commentaries, Bible dictionaries, and texts dealing with life in New Testament times may be used (see Suggested Resources).

When all the investigations are completed, have the group share the information gathered and, using the chalk board or newsprint, develop a profile of the person under study, listing all the facts uncovered about him and, in addition, recording any questions about him which remain unanswered. Have the group discuss these information gaps and see if some of them can be filled in with conclusions based upon the context of the known facts. For example, it is not recorded anywhere that Andrew felt inferior to his brother Simon Peter, but the information we do have about both of them gives substance to that conclusion.

Add the group's informed assumptions to the profile and, when this is completed, have the group re-read the pertinent article in *People Around Jesus,* comparing their own profile with the one given there. What additional insights about the individual have we gathered from the book? From our own research? In what ways did we agree or disagree with the author? What does our study tell us about Jesus' relationship with the person in question? What does the study tell us about Jesus' attitude toward the outer-circle people?

Talking It Over. This final discussion should focus upon the comparison of Jesus' way of dealing with casual acquaintances and our approach in similar circumstances. Jesus saw every person as a child of God to be loved and *served.* How often do we rather see people in terms of how they can be *used to serve us*? The following questions may be used to help the group evaluate the learnings of this session:

1. List the significant qualities of the "Jesus person" discovered in this study.

2. In what way or ways did Christ relate to people individually? To people in a group?

3. Identify several situations in which we must deal with similar persons. What does the study suggest about how we could or should relate to these persons?

4. What change in attitude and/or action do I need to make in my relationship with the people around me?

Part II.: Jesus with Children and Youth

Getting Started. Ask for volunteers to try to name every person in the group. When you are reasonably sure everyone can identify everyone else, divide the group into triads (groups of three) and allow five minutes for each person to share some experience since the last meeting in which he was reminded of Jesus' relationships with "followers at a distance."

Discovering the People Around Us. Distribute blank pieces of paper. Ask each person to make four columns on the page and label them as indicated:

Pre-Adolescent		**Teen-ager**	
Qualities		Qualities	
I admire	I dislike	I admire	I dislike

Allow about five minutes for all persons to list as many qualities as they can that they admire or dislike in both pre-adolescents and teen-agers.

When everyone has finished the listing, let each person share what he/she has written and make a composite list of the qualities named. On what items does the whole group agree? On what items is there minor disagreement? Are there any items on which the group is seriously divided? Allow the discussion to focus on "why we do not always see the desirable or undesirable qualities in exactly the same way."

Ask the participants to turn the paper over and to write the name of one child each knows exceptionally well. (It may be their own child, a neighbor, a niece or nephew, or a grandchild.) If there are young people in the group have them write the name of a brother, sister, or very close friend.

Stress that what they are about to write will not have to be shared with any other individual, and in the discussion which follows be sure you keep that promise of confidentiality, allowing them to contribute only that information which they really want to share; then ask each person to write a missing person's report on this child, giving a complete physical description and a description of the clothing worn when last seen.

NOTE: It is surprising how little we really look at the persons closest to us and how rapidly outdated our information may become on someone in the growing years. Encourage the group members to talk about how they felt trying to write this information. Was it hard or easy? Were they sure or uncertain about their facts? Encourage them to check out the information when they see the young person again. Allow them to talk briefly about why we are frequently oblivious to changes in each other, even within the same family and under the same roof.

Ask each person to write four things he/she genuinely enjoys about the child named and also four annoying things about the child. When all group members have finished writing, ask them to look over all the lists they have made concerning children and to place a small check mark beside those traits which they feel are similar to characteristics which they also possess. Do not encourage the group to a "confession" of their own traits; rather, press for a discussion of more important questions: "Do we tend to admire those qualities which make another person more like ourselves? Are we most annoyed by those traits in others which we dislike in ourselves? How can we learn to relate in more positive ways to persons who display qualities which we dislike or cannot admire? How patient and understanding are we with changes which take place as the child becomes the adolescent?

Searching the Scriptures—The Search-question Method. Have the group members select the child or youth they wish to study and write the suggested texts (texts appear on the first page of each *People* story) on a chalk board or piece of newsprint. In the whole group, take ten minutes to read over each text in silence. Encourage the use of various translations. The convener should participate fully in the entire exercise. Appoint a recorder whose task it will be to write down the search questions which the group raises.

Two categories of questions will be gathered. First have the group call out all the words or phrases in the study texts which they do not understand or which may have different meanings. As the words are called, the recorder will list them on the board. Go through the passages, verse by verse, gathering every word about which questions are raised.

For the second list of questions, ask the group to imagine itself in the situation described in the study passage: at the feeding of the multitude, in the crowd when the rich young man came to Jesus, a passer-by when Nathanael was called. In this imagination exercise, ask the group to think of questions they might have about the person or about the incident if they were present. Stimulate their fantasy with such questions as: What is the person's home life like? What occurred just before the event recorded in scripture? Just after? Why is the person in question at that place at just that time? How do the other people around him react to his confrontation with Jesus? Who are some of these other people? Can they name them? When they put themselves into the event, how do they feel about it? Does it seem strange, unfair, unbelievable, or what you might expect? Accept all questions about the text's situation, no matter how unlikely they may seem. Make certain that the recorder lists them all.

When you feel that all possible questions have been recorded, divide the group into two or three smaller groups, depending on its size. Assign an equal number of search questions from each category to each of the small groups. Provide concordances, Bible dictionaries (especially for the word study), and commentaries to assist the small groups in finding answers. Stress the fact that some answers may come not from resource texts but from personal insights and understandings of the group members and that these should be included among the answers provided.

Allow enough time for the small groups to do this research. Then, back in the whole group, receive reports from each of the small groups. Have the recorder write down the questions that still remain after the whole group has discussed the passage. Also record information and answers which the group discovers it had not thought to ask about.

When all questions have been answered and reviewed, have the group members read the *People* article in question, comparing their own questions and answers with the concerns taken up by the author.

Talking It Over. Jesus came to children and young people with the same kind of respect for their individuality which he accorded grown-ups. He gave them status as persons. Discuss this characteristic of Jesus and share in an honest evaluation of its presence among most adults and especially those in your group.

Think back over the characteristics of Jesus which the group discovered in the first session. List these from memory on a large piece of newsprint or chart paper. Add any additional qualities discovered in this session. Post the list in a conspicuous place in your meeting area, and add to the list at the end of each session.

Ask members of the group to get a mental picture of someone they feel is "good with children and/or youth." Let one person make a list on the board or a piece of chart paper as others call out one-word descriptions of the qualities which make this person "good with children and youth."

Next ask the group to develop a mental image of someone who is "not good with children or youth." Again, make a composite list of one-word descriptions.

NOTE: Don't push for a long list in either case. Let the words be spontaneous and keep them moving quickly; when the group begins to have to struggle for words, move on to the next part of the activity.

Distribute 3-by-5 cards. Ask all persons to honestly list three characteristics from the first list, "Good with . . . ," which they feel they possess. Reassure the group members that they will not be asked to share what they are writing, but do encourage them to actually write it down, not just think about it. Allow enough time for reflection and writing. Then ask the group to select three qualities from either list that they would like to work on in their own relationships with children and to write these on the cards. Suggest that the cards be tucked in each person's wallet and referred to from time to time until the person feels he or she is actually making progress toward a more positive relationship with young people.

If this activity has been meaningful for the group, it might be appropriate to close with shared-sentence prayers.

Part III.: The Sick and the Sorrowing

Getting Started. If there are newcomers, welcome them as the group is gathering and introduce them one or two at a time to the other members of the group before the meeting begins. When everyone has arrived, take a few moments to reflect on the things done and the discoveries made in the previous sessions by asking members of the group to indicate:

1. What parts of the study have been most fun?
2. What has been the most interesting discovery?
3. What has raised the most questions for you?

4. What new insights have you gained which have influenced the way you have related to others since the study began?

Discovering the People Around Us. We are all sympathetic and concerned about the sick and the sorrowing people around us. But most of us are extremely uneasy and self-conscious when it comes to dealing with them face to face. What do you say? What can you do? How can you really cheer them? Do we avoid confrontations with them? Are we overindulgent?

Divide the group into threes. List the following situations on the chalk board and ask the group to add any others which they would like to consider in this study:

—a hospital visit to a young man seriously injured in an automobile accident.

—a condolence call to the funeral home to visit an elderly man whose wife has died after a long illness.

—a home visit to a young girl home from college to recover from mono.

—a visit to a bereaved mother whose child has suddenly died.

—a hospital visit to see a close friend who just gave birth to her fourth child.

—grandparents visiting a twelve-year-old who just broke his leg.

—a visit to a long-term resident of a nursing home.

—an unexpected visit from a friend who has been recently divorced.

—luncheon with a friend whose doctor has just recommended surgery for a possible cancer.

Let each triad select one situation to role-play. Give them a few minutes to talk over the situation, adding any pertinent facts they need. Arrange the chairs in a circle, placing three in the center for the role-play participants. To avoid discussion of the situations until all have been enacted, distribute pencils and paper to all members of the group and at the end of each role play ask them to list briefly the strengths and weaknesses they observed in each encounter. When all role-play situations have been presented, let the discussion focus on a sharing of the lists, with emphasis on the positive things individuals can do in confronting the sick and sorrowing. Avoid criticism of the role-playing itself; the quality of acting is unimportant and a group may have deliberately chosen to illustrate how *not* to deal with an encounter of this kind.

Have the triads share their reasons for choosing the particular situation they portrayed. Was it easier? Less threatening than the others? Had they had a recent experience in a similar situation? Did it recall a personal experience?

Ask the whole group to reflect on the possible reasons for avoiding some role-play situations. Do we tend to avoid the same situations in real life? Why? Why not? How can we develop a feeling of confidence in dealing with these situations?

Searching the Scriptures—Personal-translation Method. Select the person or persons to be studied and assign the prescribed texts to small groups for study and translation. Have each person in the small group *write* his own version of the passage under study. They will do this independently of one another. When the process is completed, members of the small groups will share their translations, selecting the clearest and most articulate expressions for their group translation of the passage.

In discussing the different translations, the group will take up the various shades of meaning which the passage offers. When differences of opinion about a given text arise, they should be resolved by consulting commentaries and other resources. The small group's final translation should be read to the whole group as members read the same passage again in their preferred translations. When this has been done, participants will again read the *People* article under study, comparing its "version" with the translations they have done. What added insight does the "homemade" translation add to the passage? Does it distort the original in any way? What new information do we have about Jesus and the person under study?

Talking It Over. As time permits, have the group members compare some of their earlier role-play attitudes and reactions toward the sick and troubled people around them with those of the Christ in similar circumstances. How can his approach become a more realistic part of our own practice?

Part IV.: Jesus and Women

Getting Started. You are now past the halfway mark in your six-session study. Has the complexion of your group changed much since the first session? Is it larger? Smaller? Are there different people every week? How well do the members of the group relate to one another? Has this discussion of Jesus' relationships with people had a visible effect upon the interpersonal relationships of group members? Start this session with an informal discussion of questions like these.

Discovering the People Around Us. No matter how "open" we profess to be, our preconceived notion of what is proper often deprives women of individual personhood, contrary to Jesus' way of openness and his objective acceptance of every person in his and her own right.

Distribute several 3-by-5 cards to each person in the group. Place an additional stack of cards in a convenient place for anyone who needs more during the activity. On a chalk board write these two incomplete sentences:

"Women should..."
"Women should not..."

Ask each participant to write as many statements as he can think of—one to each card—each beginning with either of these phrases.

Allow at least five minutes for the writing—longer if most of the group is actively involved. When everyone has finished, collect all the cards. Shuffle them several times to mix them up and then deal them out one at a time around the group until all the cards are redistributed. Let members of the group read the cards in their possession, beginning with those which state, "Women should..." A lively debate will spontaneously ensue. Remind the group that it is not necessary to identify who wrote the card unless the person wishes it. Make no attempt to referee the discussion, but be sensitive to the need to stay on the subject and do not let the discussion wander or degenerate into a heated argument between two or more individuals.

Before going on to the searching of the scriptures, reflect briefly on Jesus' quality of openness and his objective acceptance of every person in his or her own right as illustrated in previous session studies. Add any qualities to the list begun in Session Two which the group feels is appropriate.

Searching the Scriptures—Choose Your Method. Three different Bible-study methods have been described in this guide thus far. If all three have been used, it will be best now to choose that one which the group finds most helpful and with which it feels most comfortable. The three methods, Resources-study,

Search-questions, and Personal-translation, all lend themselves to a small-group shared study. Let the group decide which method it prefers and refer back as necessary to the appropriate guidance material for searching the scriptures in this session. (Resources-study Method, p. 115; Search-question Method, p. 118; Personal-translation Method, p. 122.)

Talking It Over. In light of your study, what do you think Jesus' approach to women would be today? What additional characteristics of the Christ have you discovered which should be added to the list begun in Session Two?

Refer to the lists of "shoulds" and "should nots" compiled in the earlier activity. Which five issues do you think Jesus would give highest priority for women today? Let the discussion continue until the group has agreed on the top five. Are there any issues which you feel the Christ would treat as superficial or petty? Which of these issues were also concerns to the women of his day? In what ways has your understanding of the crucial issues of women today been affected by this study?

Part V.: The Outsiders

Getting Started. Your group has no doubt begun to feel and enjoy its own identity. You have been studying and talking together about the Word of God and its relevance for your own personal relationships and interpersonal involvements. You will not need to spend much time on preliminaries, but once again, make certain that everyone is acquainted. If there are questions or comments left hanging from previous sessions, they ought to be considered before going on.

Discovering the People Around Us. We all have certain people who "rub us the wrong way," people with whom we must work or live as neighbors on the same street or in the same apartment house. How does a Christian deal with these people? Can a Christ-follower love his neighbor without really liking him?

In many ways this is a very personal matter, so take time for some quiet, individual reflection before going into the search of the scriptures. Have the group members take a piece of paper, ruling four columns on it. At the top of the first two columns write the names of two persons they genuinely like and with whom they get along well.

On a chalk board or chart paper write the following questions and let each person answer them in the columns below the two names:

—on what occasions are we together?
—what interests do we share in common?
—who usually initiates our getting together?
—what significant experiences have we shared?
—what are this person's greatest concerns or needs?
—what have I done recently to be of help to this person?

When the group members have had time to complete the first two columns, ask them to write in the remaining two columns the names of two persons they genuinely dislike and with whom they do not get along well. Again ask each person to silently write the answers to the same questions below the names of those who "rub them the wrong way." Reassure them that they will not be asked to share any personal information. This is for their own self-study.

Allow enough time for individuals to think about the questions in depth and to write the information requested. Then open the possibility for discussion by asking:

—what did you discover in this process?
—did anything surprise you?
—did it suggest anything about the reasons we tend to like or dislike other persons?
—whom do we tend to know better, persons we like or persons we dislike?
—toward whom do we tend to show more concern?

Searching the Scriptures. Select the person or persons to be studied. As in the previous session, use the study method chosen by the group, referring to the guidance material provided in the previous sessions as necessary. (Resources-study Method, p. 115; Search-question Method, p. 118; Personal-translation Method, p. 122.) Regardless of the method chosen, continue to encourage the use of commentaries, dictionaries, and other resource materials.

Talking It Over. This should be an in-depth sharing experience in which the members of the group have the opportunity to talk over their own frustrations over disagreements with disagreeable people and in which the compassionate, forgiving love of Christ is examined and evaluated in a forthright way. Can you really forgive and forget? Can an antagonistic foe ever become a true and trusted friend? How realistic is Christ's command to love one's enemies?

Part VI.: Disciples-Come-Lately

Getting Started. In this final session it may be helpful for the group members to chat informally about some of the things they have learned about one another in the give and take of this study. Have former strangers become acquainted? Has casual acquaintance deepened into friendship? What one point of recall stands out about each member of the group? Has the personal image of any of the other persons changed as a result of association in this study? This exercise is meant to measure the degree of familiarity achieved in the group during the six weeks of the study.

Discovering the People Around Us. Distribute three 3-by-5 cards to each person. On the first card have all persons list two things they really enjoy doing when they have time. On the second card ask them to write two things they feel they do really well in their everyday work. (And don't let young people or full-time homemakers cop out; homemaking is creative work of the first water, and young people *work* if they are in school.) Take up the first two cards from each person, shuffle them, and redistribute them to the group. (The third card is set aside for the moment.) Next post several large sheets of chart paper on the wall and get one or two volunteers to serve as recorders for a brainstorming session. Appoint one person with a second hand on his watch to be timekeeper. One at a time let members of the group read an interest or talent from their cards. As soon as the interest or talent is named, record it on the chart paper and give the group exactly two minutes to call out as many ways as they can in which this interest or talent could be used to enhance a Christ-spirit within the church and the community.

Let the timekeeper keep strict control and move on quickly to the next talent. One basic rule must be followed: record every idea no matter how strange, far-out, or silly it sounds. No one is allowed to criticize or discuss someone else's idea at this time. The object is to get as many ideas as possible on the chart papers in the time allowed. Encourage piggy-backing ideas—that is, expanding upon or using a previous idea as a take-off point for a new one.

When all the talents and interests have been brainstormed, ask each person to read, silently and carefully, the lists of ideas for his own particular talents, and then take the third card and complete the following sentence:

> To further enhance a Christ-spirit within the church and in this community, I will ___(do something specific)___ starting ___(when)___ .

By this time the group members should feel free enough with each other to be comfortable in sharing what they have written on the third card. Allow this to happen if at all possible. Don't force the issue if the group is still reluctant to share personal information. Allow the group to think through the difference between being able to stand up for Christ as Paul did, saying, "*This* I will do," and the self-effacing "I don't really do anything well enough to tell others about it."

Searching the Scriptures. The scriptural study of Paul will use the method preferred by the group. It should be said, however, that with the wealth of material available in most New Testament commentaries, the Resources-study Method (p. 115) may be most effective for this session. The group should also read the two essays in the "Disciples-Come-Lately" section of this book.

Keep in mind that your primary purpose in this scriptural study is to show how a relationship with Christ may change a person's direction, but it does not necessarily alter the dynamics of his creative personality and life-style. A converted Christian has a new motivating force driving him. He is the same person with the same gifts and skills and many of the same weaknesses and idiosyncrasies, but his life's purpose has shifted its center from himself to the Lord Jesus Christ.

Talking It Over. It will be important for the group to spend these final few moments in an evaluation of the learnings they have shared about the person of Jesus—what was he really like? —and the new insights they have gained about themselves as the people around Jesus today.

About the Author

Walter A. Kortrey is pastor of Christ's Lutheran Church, Woodstock, New York. A graduate of Wagner College and the Lutheran Theological Seminary at Philadelphia, he has been pastor of Gloria Dei Lutheran Church, New Hyde Park, New York, and Trinity Lutheran Church, Lansdale, Pennsylvania. From 1962 to 1969 he was an editor for the Lutheran Church of America's Board of Parish Education. He has published articles in a number of periodicals including *The Lutheran, Lutheran Women,* and *The Christian Century.*